BIG-NOTE PIANO

S0-BFD-111

THE BIG-NOTE
Christmas Collection

ISBN 0-634-04754-X

HAL•LEONARD®
CORPORATION

7777 W. BLUEMOUND RD. P.O. BOX 13819 MILWAUKEE, WI 53213

Visit Hal Leonard Online at
www.halleonard.com

CONTENTS

ANGELS WE HAVE HEARD ON HIGH

Traditional French Carol
Translated by JAMES CHADWICK

An - gels we have heard on high sweet - ly sing - ing
o'er the plains, And the moun - tains in re - ply
Ech - o - ing their joy - ous strains. Glo -
- ri - a in ex - cel - sis

AWAY IN A MANGER

Traditional
Words by JOHN T. McFARLAND (v.3)
Music by JAMES R. MURRAY

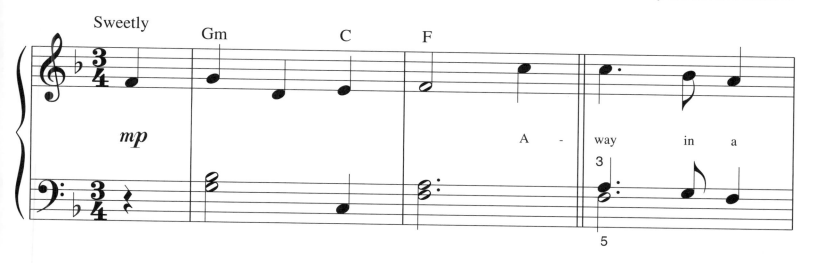

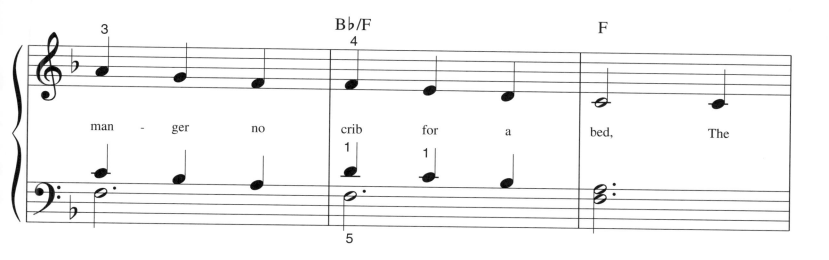

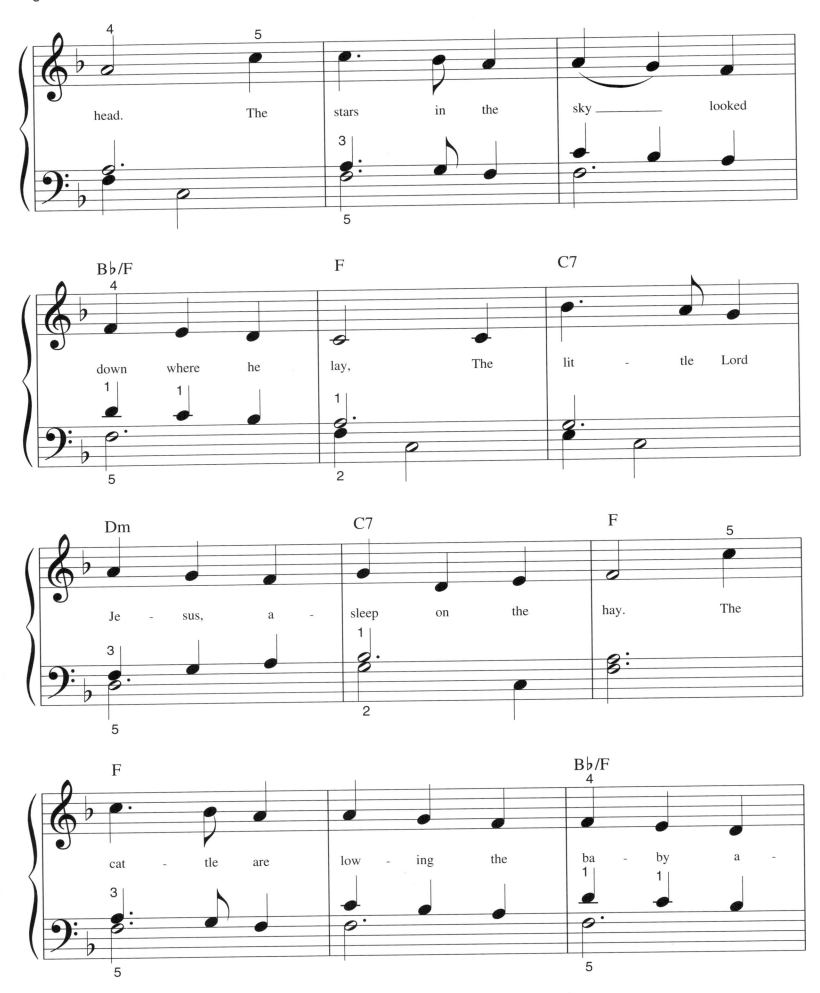

As Long As There's Christmas

from Walt Disney's BEAUTY AND THE BEAST - THE ENCHANTED CHRISTMAS

Music by RACHEL PORTMAN
Lyrics by DON BLACK

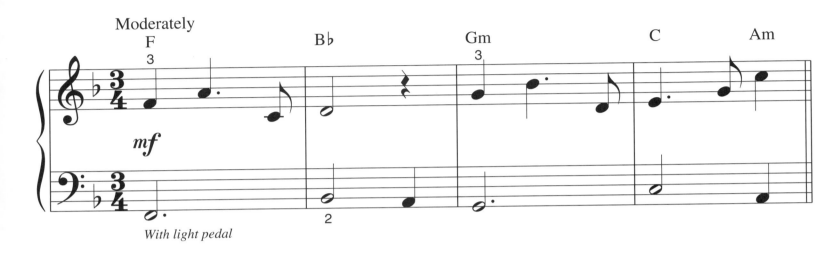

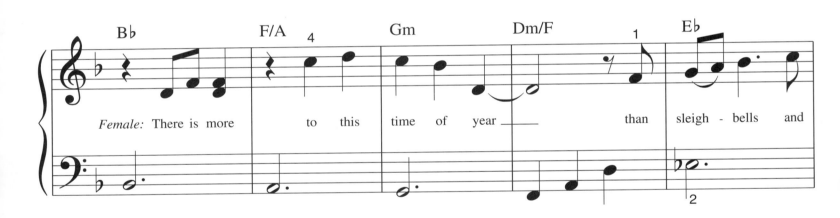

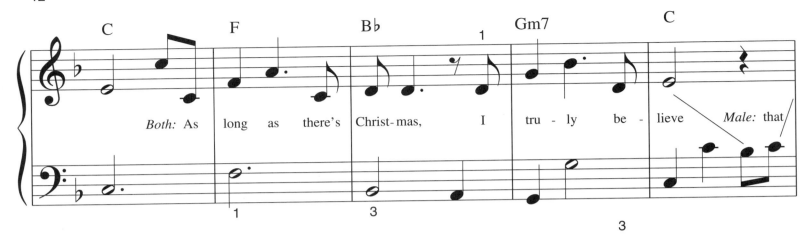

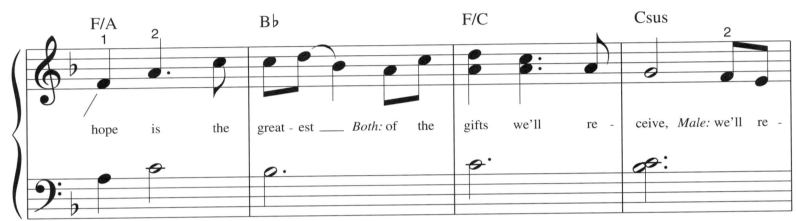

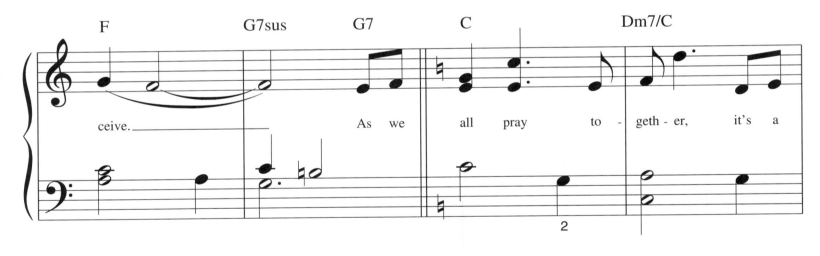

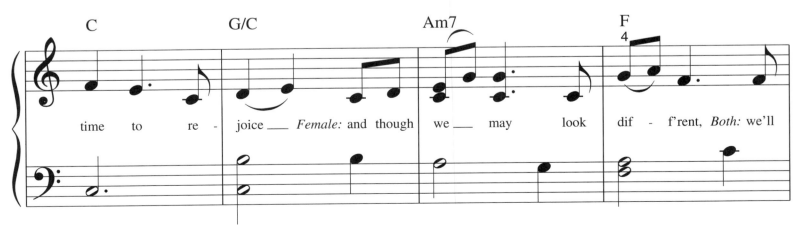

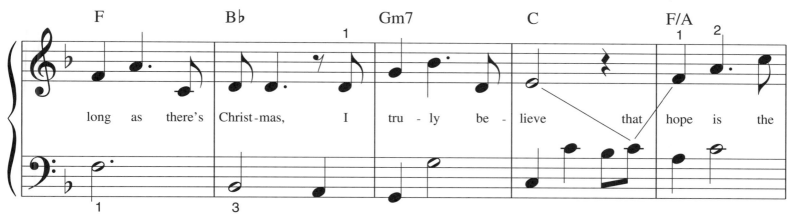

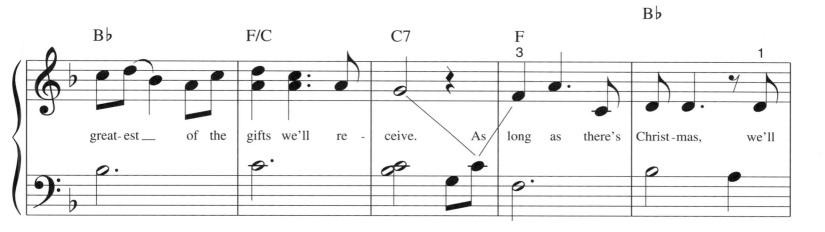

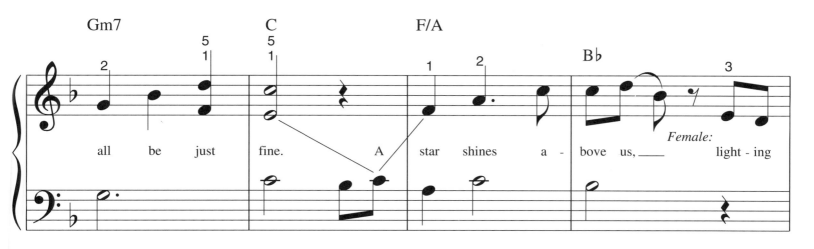

13

BECAUSE IT'S CHRISTMAS
(For All the Children)

Music by BARRY MANILOW
Lyric by BRUCE SUSSMAN and JACK FELDMAN

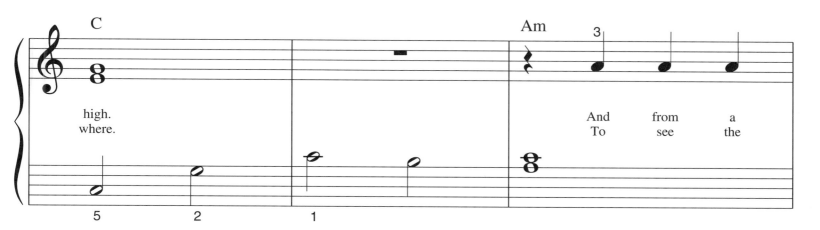

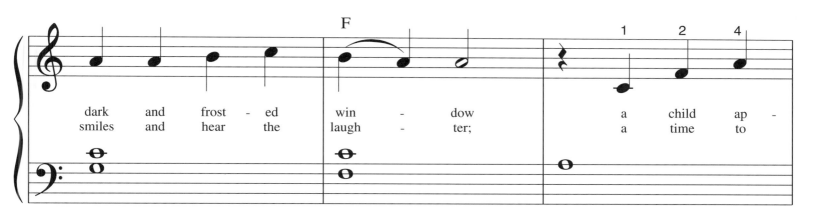

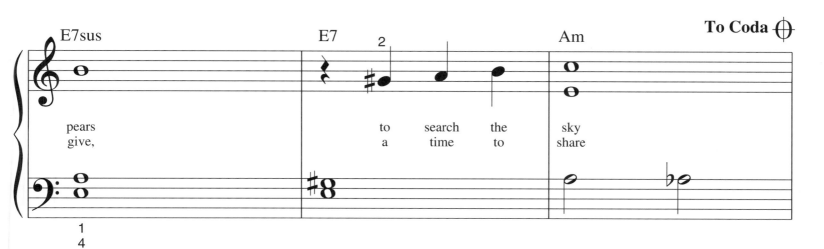

18

CODA

CAROLING, CAROLING

Words by WIHLA HUTSON
Music by ALFRED BURT

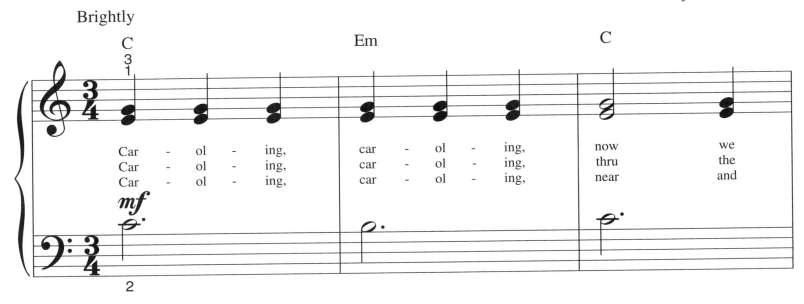

THE CHRISTMAS SONG
(Chestnuts Roasting on an Open Fire)

Music and Lyric by MEL TORME
and ROBERT WELLS

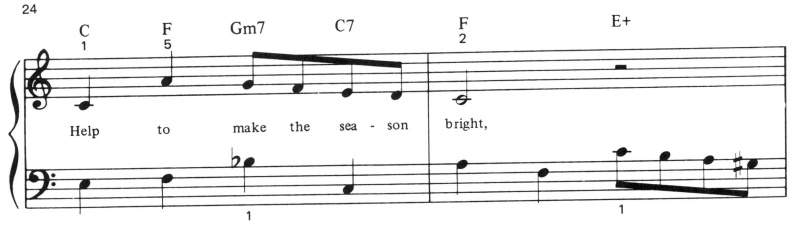

Help to make the sea - son bright,

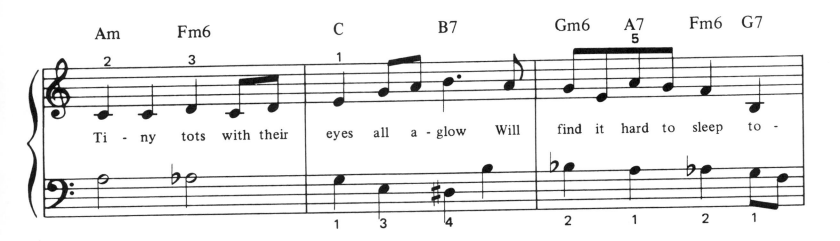

Ti - ny tots with their eyes all a - glow Will find it hard to sleep to -

night. They know that San - ta's on his way; He's load - ed

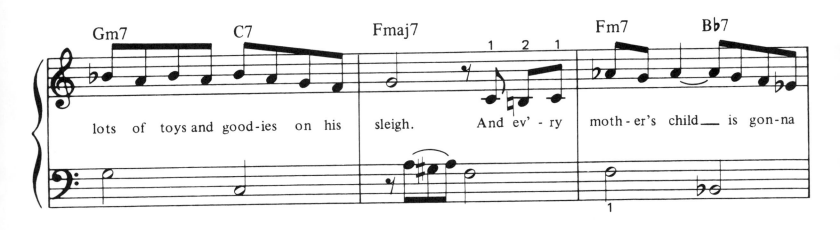

lots of toys and good-ies on his sleigh. And ev' - ry moth - er's child__ is gon-na

THE CHIPMUNK SONG

Words and Music by
ROSS BAGDASARIAN

Want a plane that loops the loop;

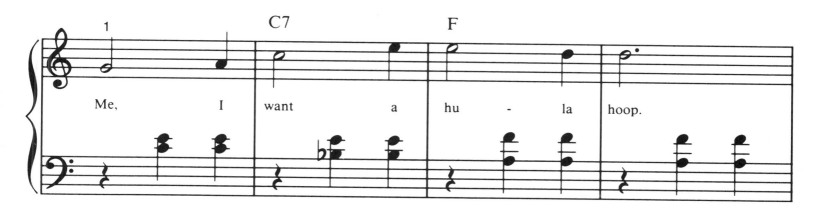

C7   F

Me, I want a hu - la hoop.

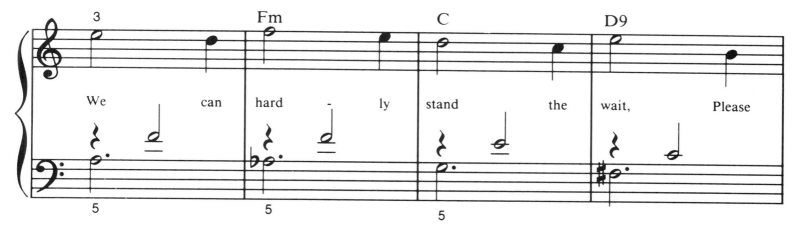

Fm   C   D9

We can hard - ly stand the wait, Please

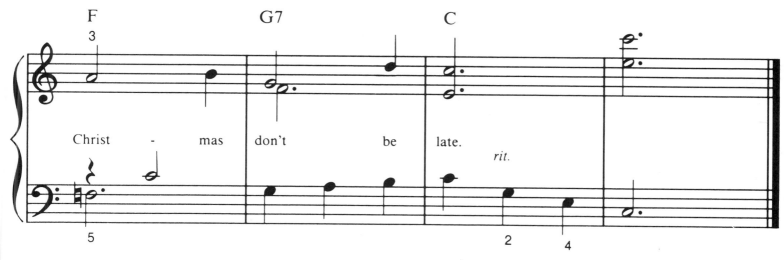

F   G7   C

Christ - mas don't be late. *rit.*

THE CHRISTMAS SHOES

Words and Music by LEONARD AHLSTROM
and EDDIE CARSWELL

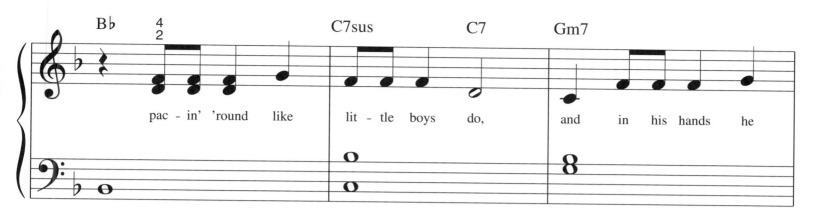

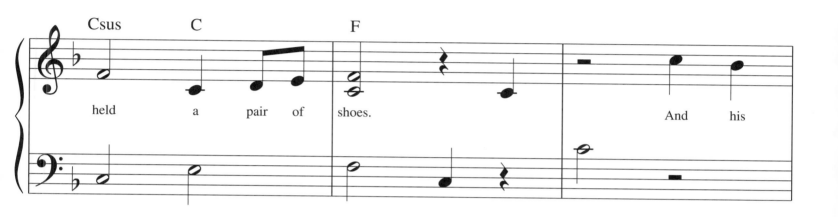

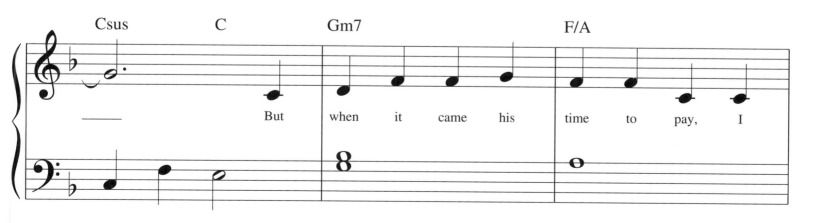

D — Dad-dy says there's not much time. — Em You see, G/D

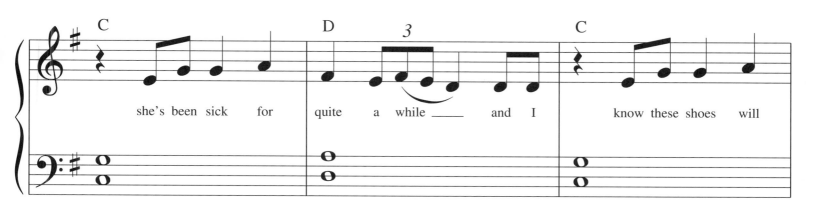

C she's been sick for D 3 quite a while — and I C know these shoes will

D 3 make her smile — and I C want her to look Dsus D beau-ti-ful if

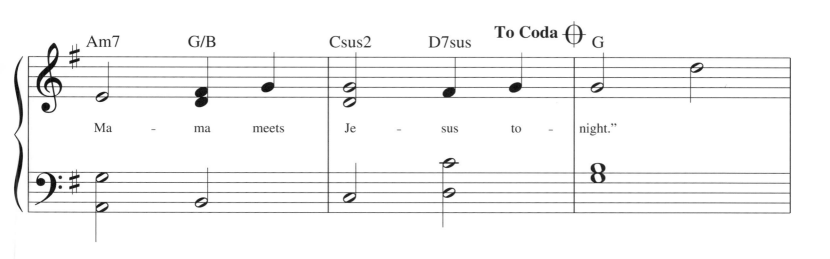

Am7 Ma - ma G/B meets Csus2 Je - sus D7sus to - **To Coda** G night."

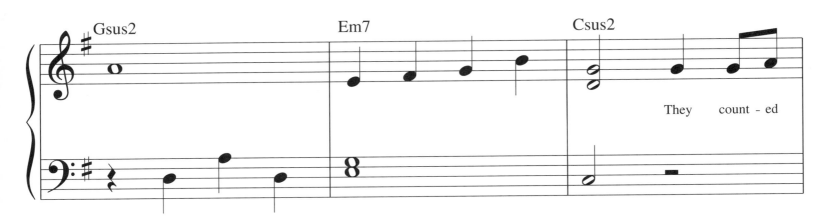

They count - ed

pen - nies for what seemed like years, then the cash - ier said, "Son, there's

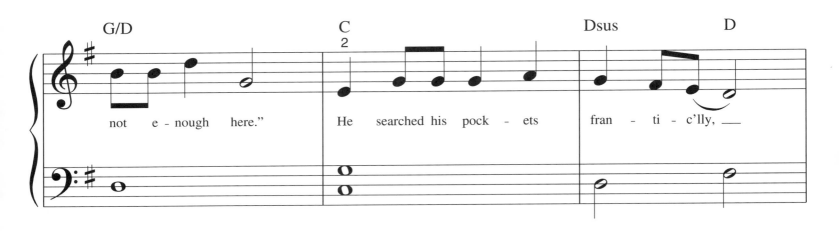

not e - nough here." He searched his pock - ets fran - ti - c'lly, ___

then he turned and he looked at me. He said, "Ma - ma made Christ - mas

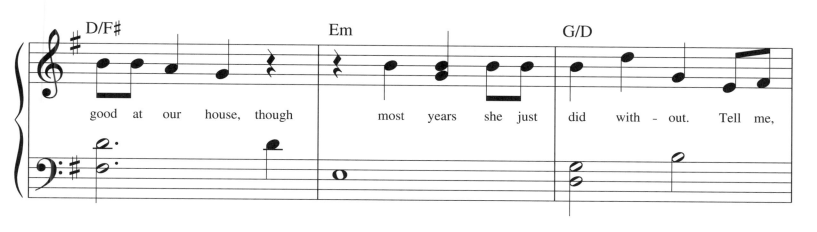

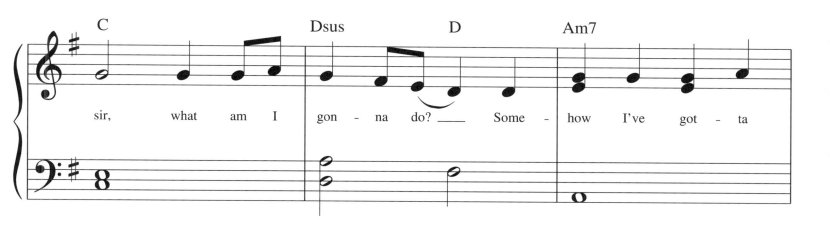

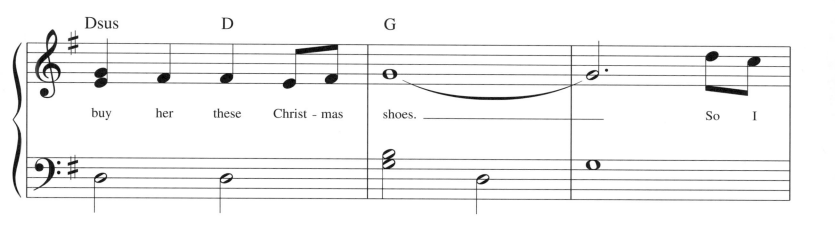

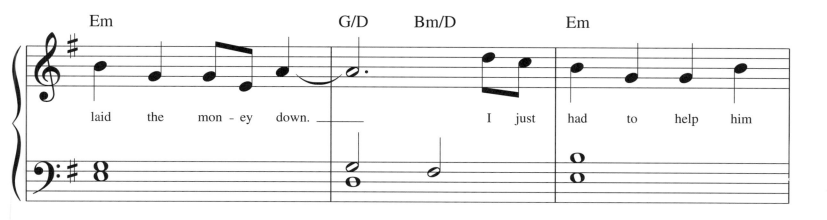

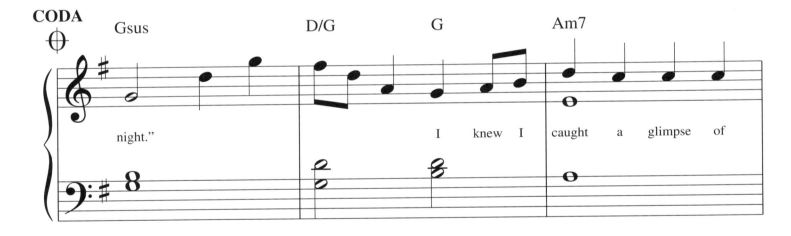

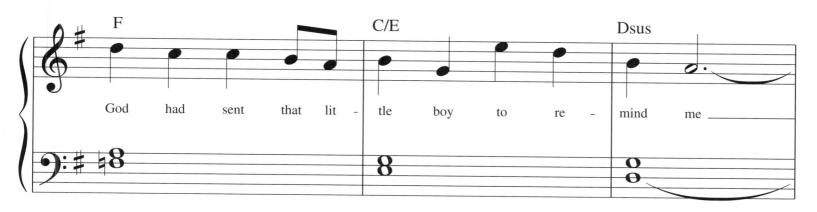

God had sent that lit - tle boy to re - mind me ___

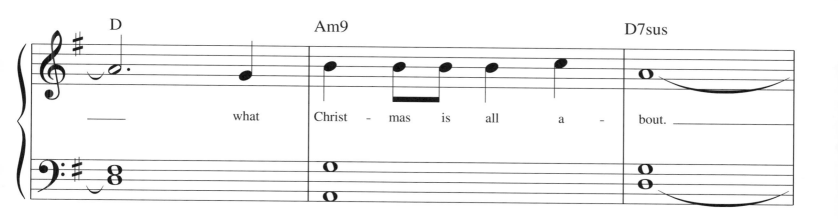

___ what Christ - mas is all a - bout. ___

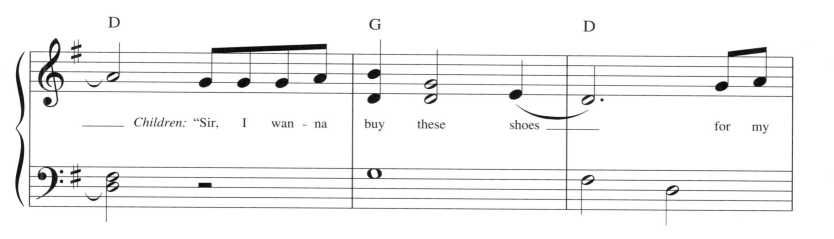

___ *Children:* "Sir, I wan - na buy these shoes ___ for my

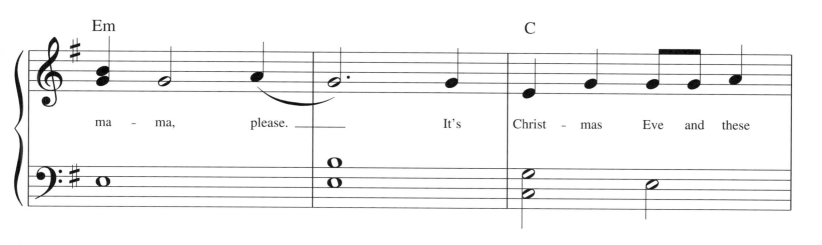

ma - ma, please. ___ It's Christ - mas Eve and these

36

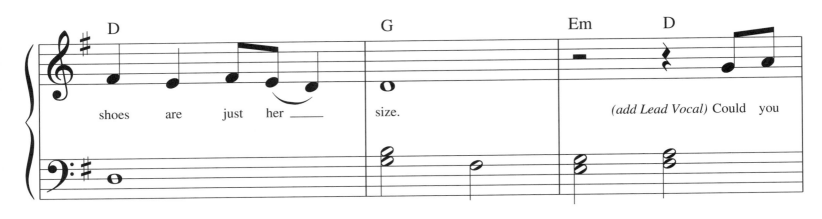

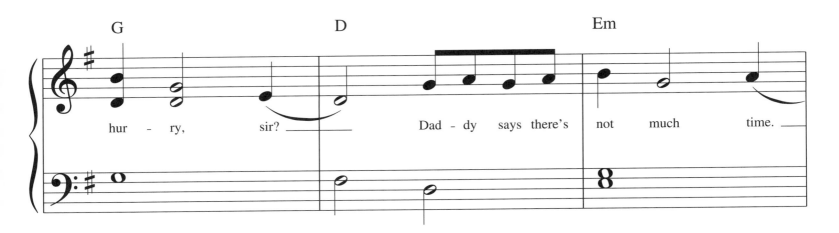

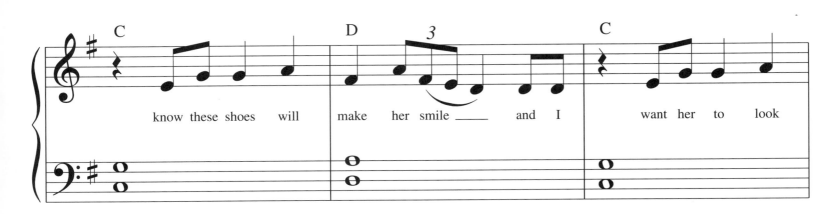

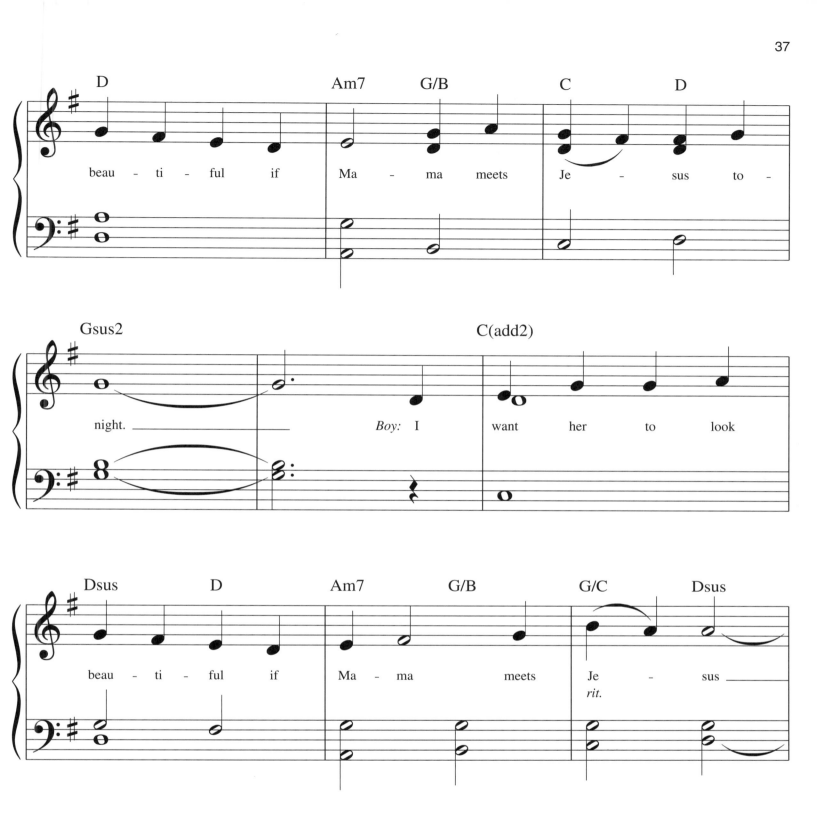

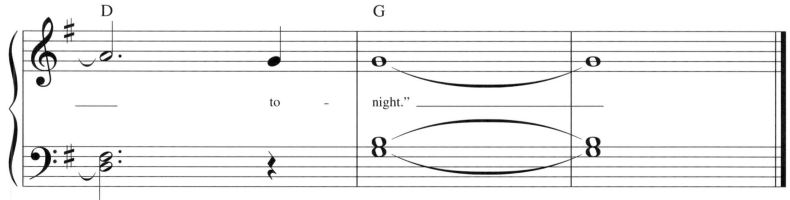

CHRISTMAS TIME IS HERE

from A CHARLIE BROWN CHRISTMAS

Words by LEE MENDELSON
Music by VINCE GUARALDI

THE CHRISTMAS WALTZ

Words by SAMMY CAHN
Music by JULE STYNE

Graceful Waltz

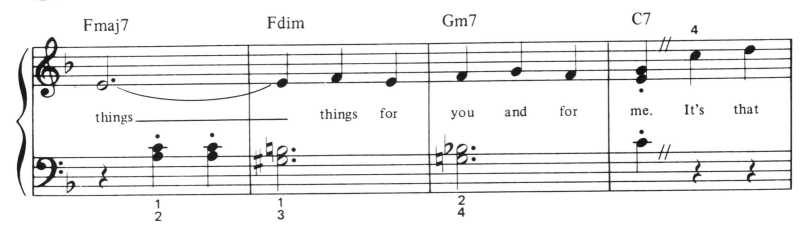

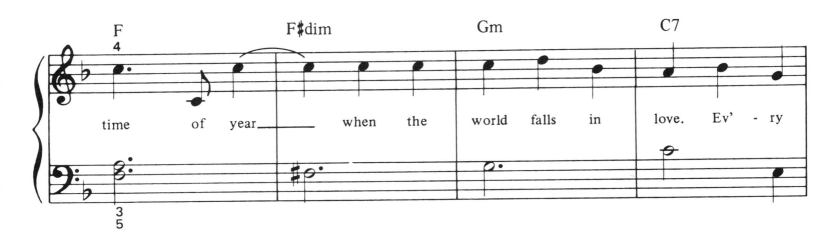

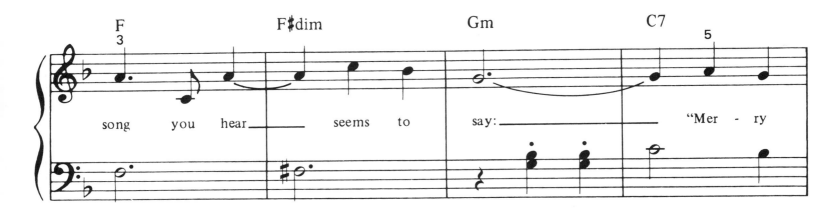

DECK THE HALL

Traditional Welsh Carol

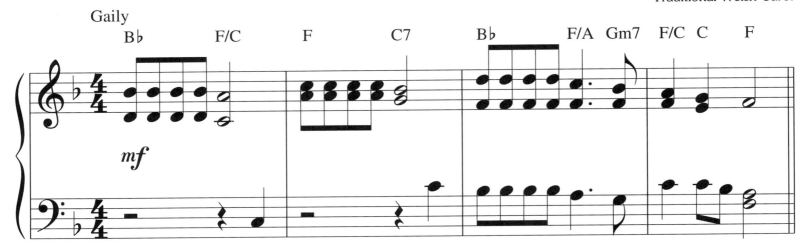

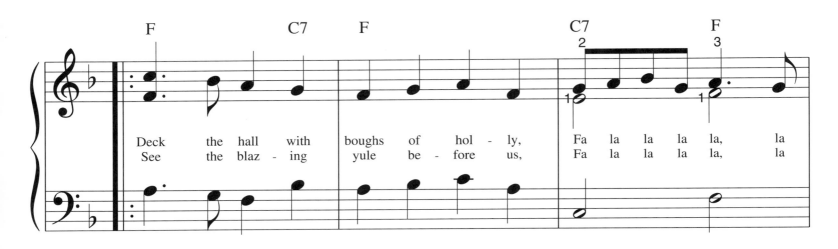

Deck the hall with boughs of hol - ly,
Fa la la la la, la la la la la.

See the blaz - ing yule be - fore us,
Fa la la la la, la la la la la.

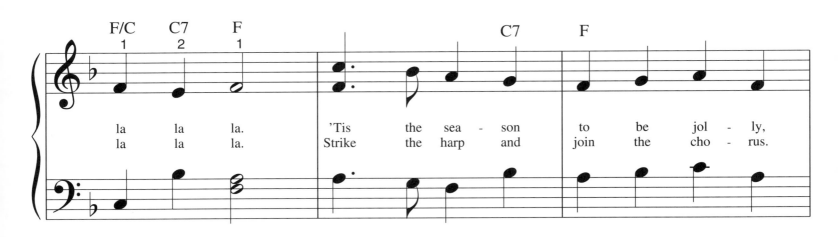

la la la. 'Tis the sea - son to be jol - ly,

la la la. Strike the harp and join the cho - rus.

DING DONG! MERRILY ON HIGH!

French Carol

Ding dong! Merrily on high in
E'en so here below, be-low, let

heav'n the bells are ring - ing.
stee - ple bells be swung - en,

Ding dong! Ver - i - ly the sky is
And i - o, i - o, i - o, by

DO THEY KNOW IT'S CHRISTMAS?

Words and Music by M. URE
and B. GELDOF

oth - er ones   at   Christ - mas

time.   It's   hard,   but   when   you're

hav - ing   fun, _____   there's   a

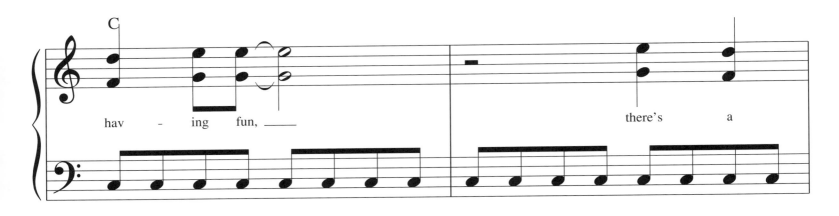

world   out - side   your   win - dow   and   it's   a   world   of   dread   and

And there won't be snow ____ in Af - ri - ca ____ this

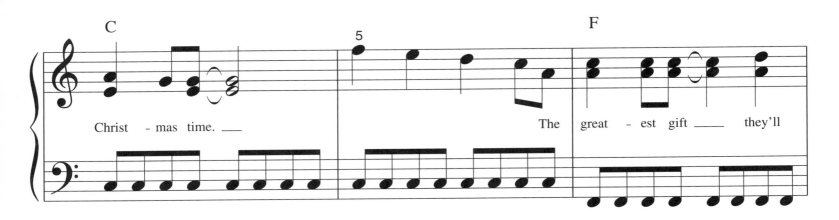

Christ - mas time. ____ The great - est gift ____ they'll

get this year ____ is life.

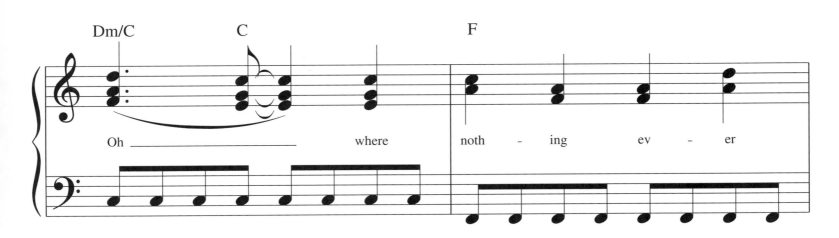

Oh _____ where noth - ing ev - er

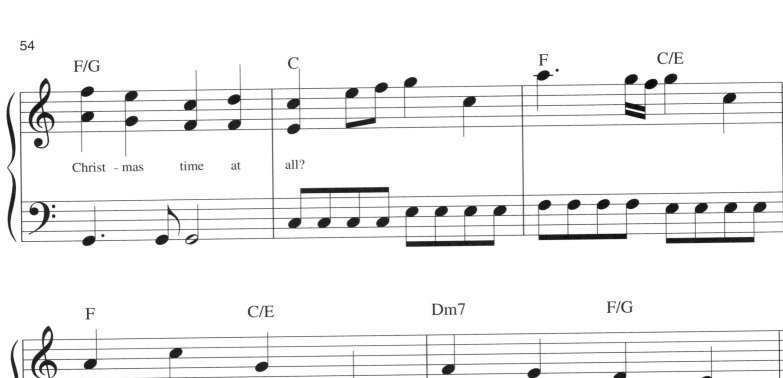

Christ - mas time at all?

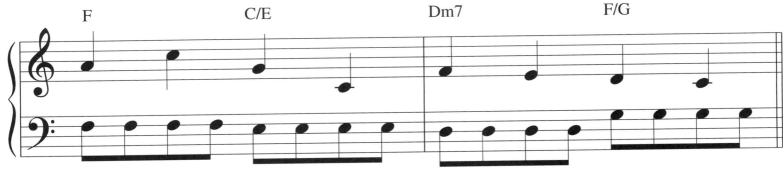

Feed the
gain.

world, _____

let them know it's

1.
Christ - mas time a -

2.
Christ - mas time a - gain.

DO YOU HEAR WHAT I HEAR

Words and Music by NOEL REGNEY
and GLORIA SHAYNE

56

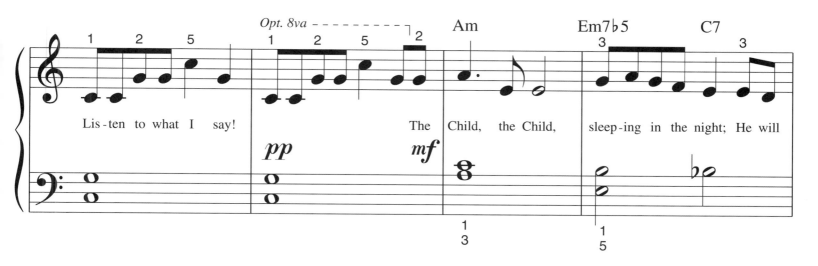

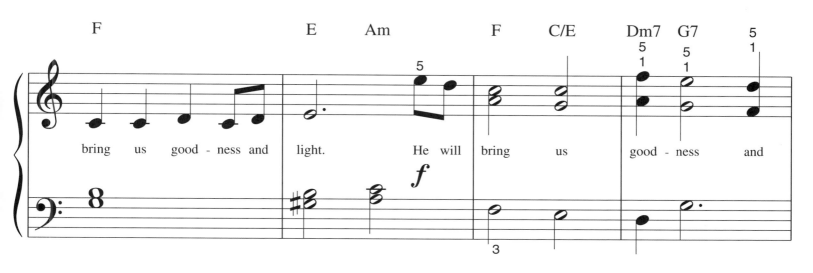

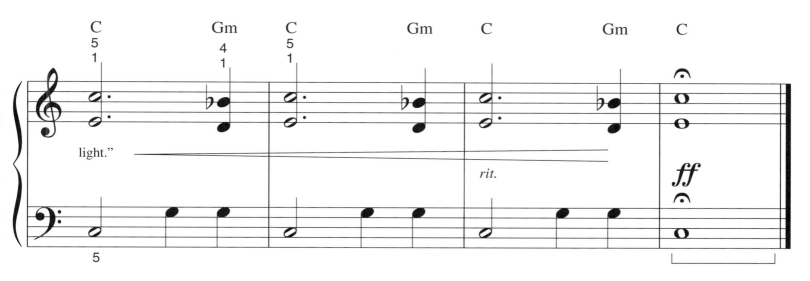

Additional Lyrics

3. Said the shepherd boy to the mighty king,
   "Do you know what I know?
   In your palace warm, mighty king,
   Do you know what I know?
   A Child, A Child shivers in the cold;
   Let us bring Him silver and gold,
   Let us bring Him silver and gold."

EMMANUEL

Words and Music by
MICHAEL W. SMITH

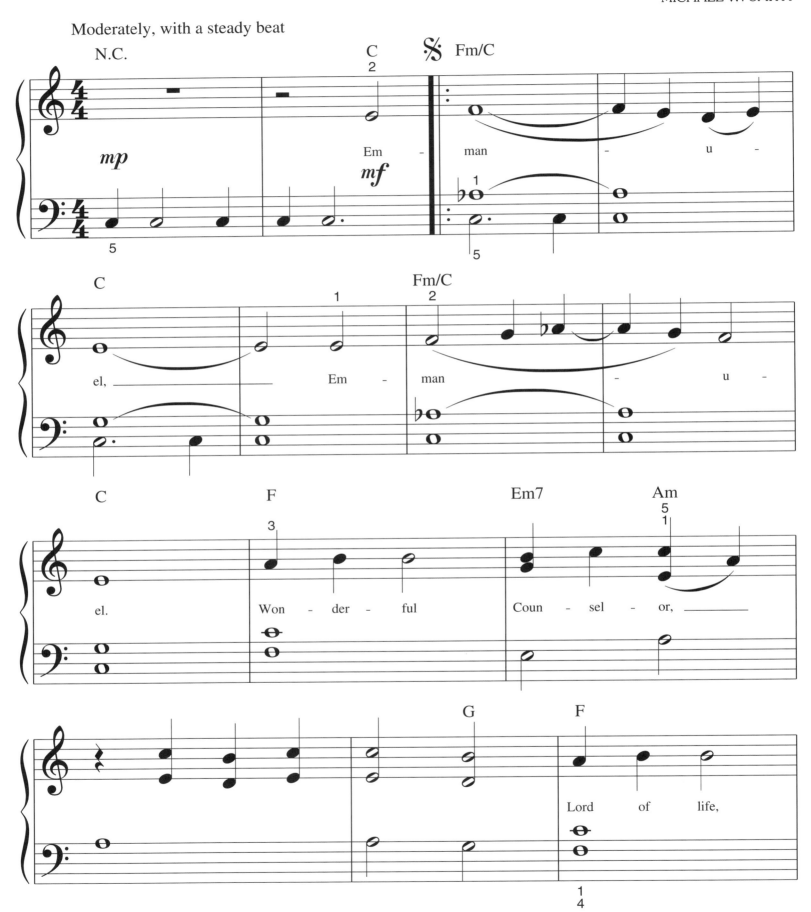

60

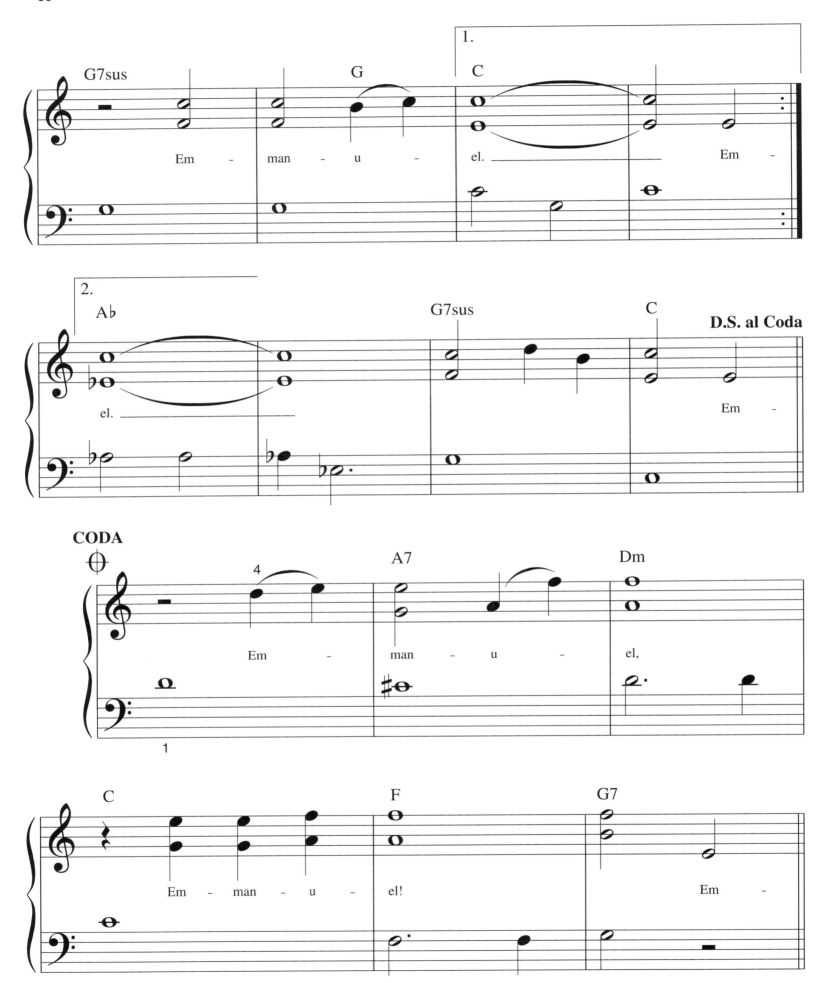

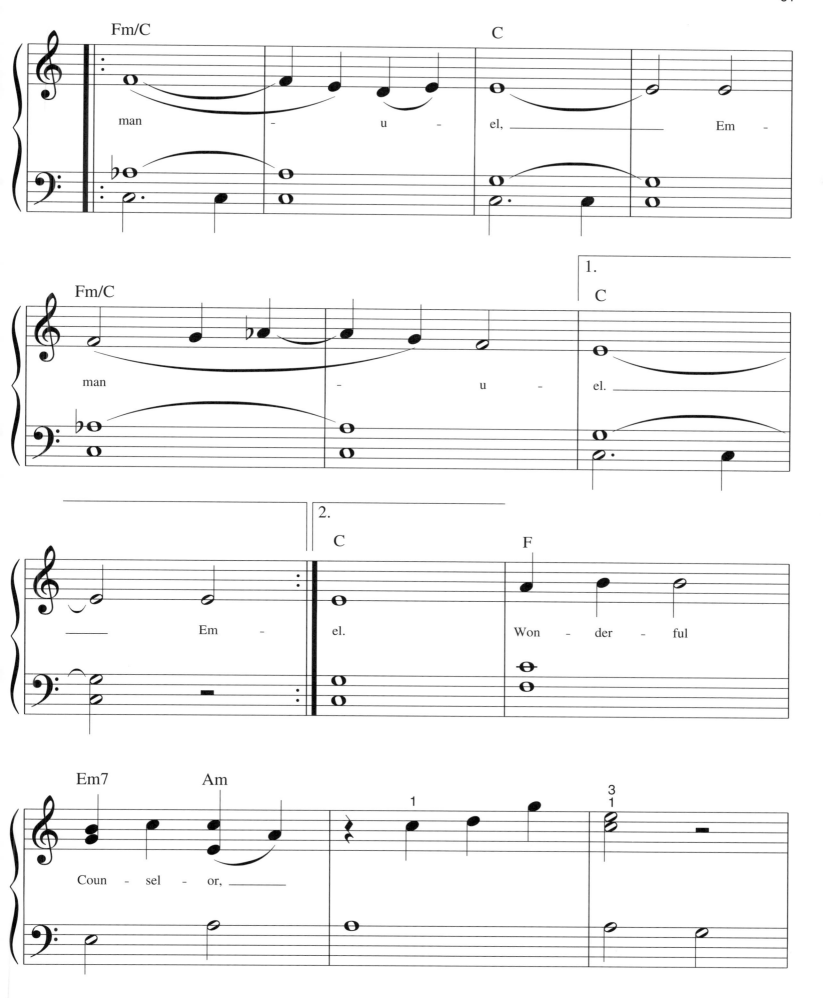

63

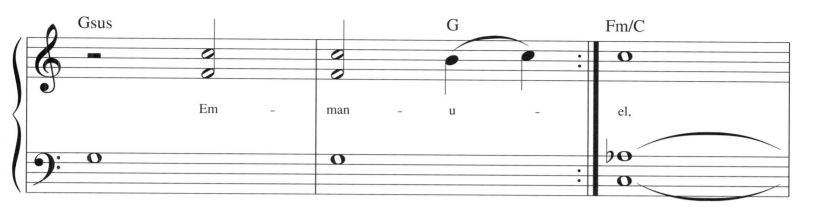

Em - man - u - el,

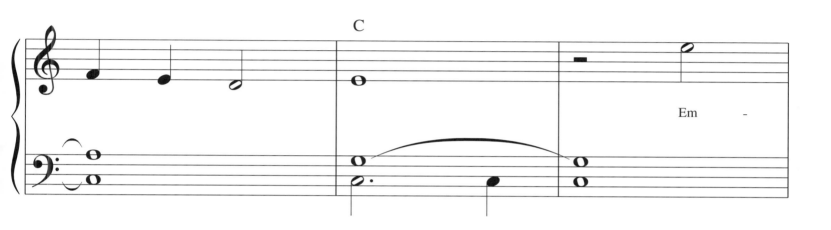

Em -

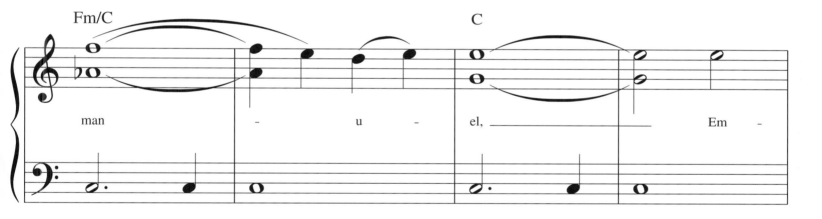

man - u - el, Em -

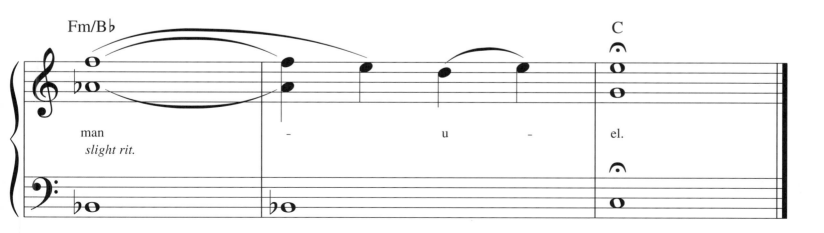

man - u - el.

slight rit.

FELIZ NAVIDAD

Music and Lyrics by
JOSÉ FELICIANO

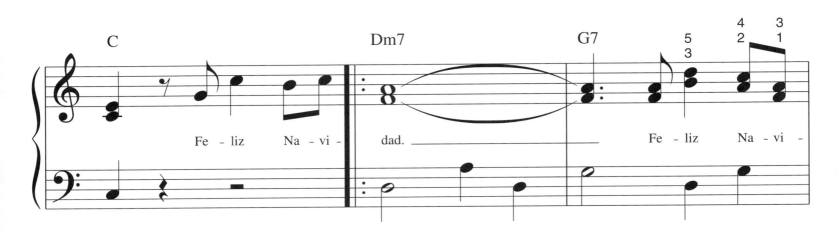

65

THE FIRST NOËL

17th Century English Carol
Music from W. Sandys' *Christmas Carols*

Moderately slow

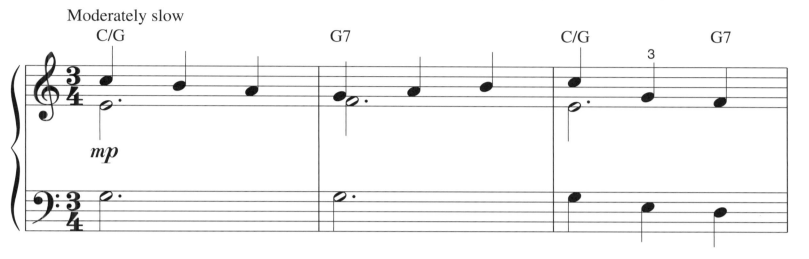

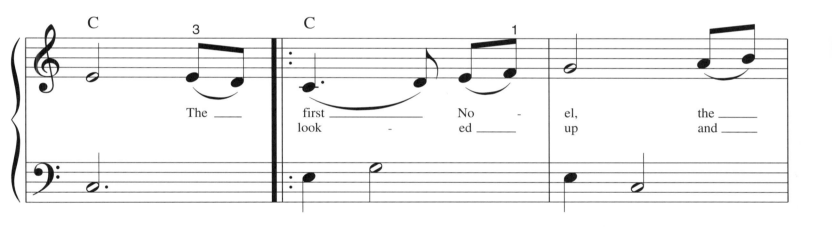

The ___ first _____ No - el, the _____
look - ed ___ up and _____

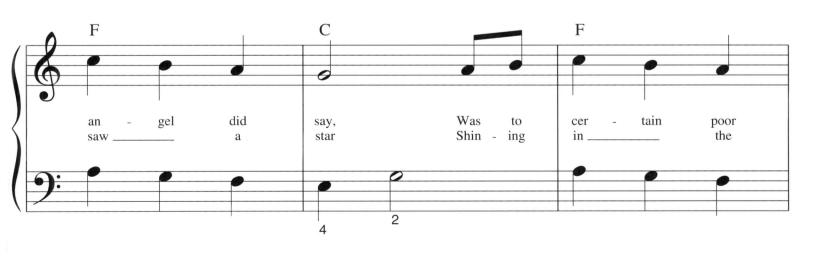

an - gel did say, Was to cer - tain poor
saw _____ a star Shin - ing in _____ the

FROSTY THE SNOW MAN

Words and Music by STEVE NELSON
and JACK ROLLINS

fair - y tale they say,
broom - stick in his hand,

He was made of snow but the
Run - ning here and there all a -

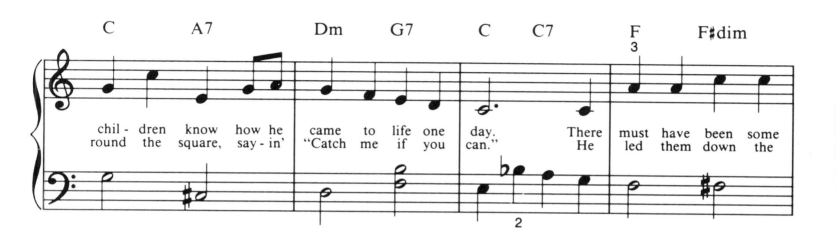

chil - dren know how he came to life one day.
round the square, say - in' "Catch me if you can."

There must have been some
He led them down the

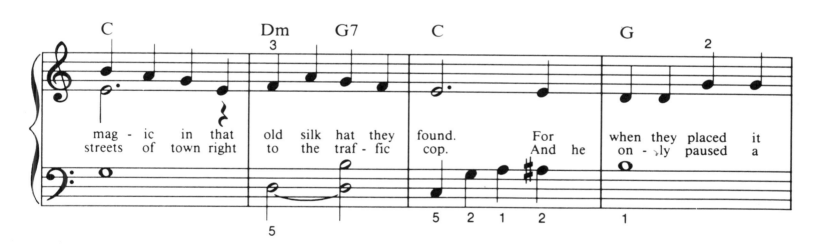

mag - ic in that old silk hat they found.
streets of town right to the traf - fic cop.

For
And he

when they placed it
on - ly paused a

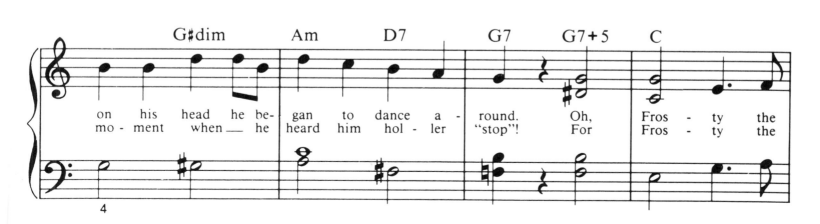

on his head he be - gan to dance a - round.
mo - ment when ___ he heard him hol - ler

Oh,
"stop"! For

Fros - ty the
Fros - ty the

72

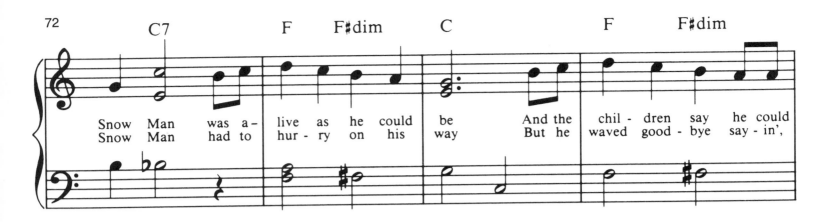

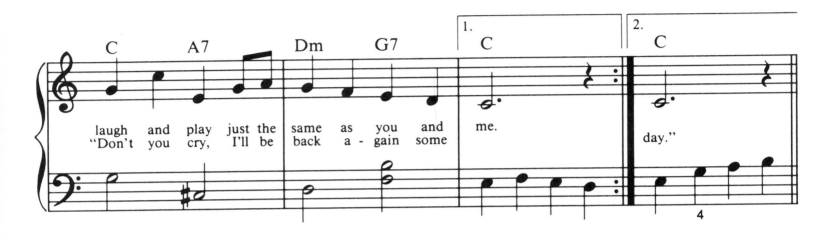

HAPPY HOLIDAY
from the Motion Picture Irving Berlin's HOLIDAY INN

Words and Music by
IRVING BERLIN

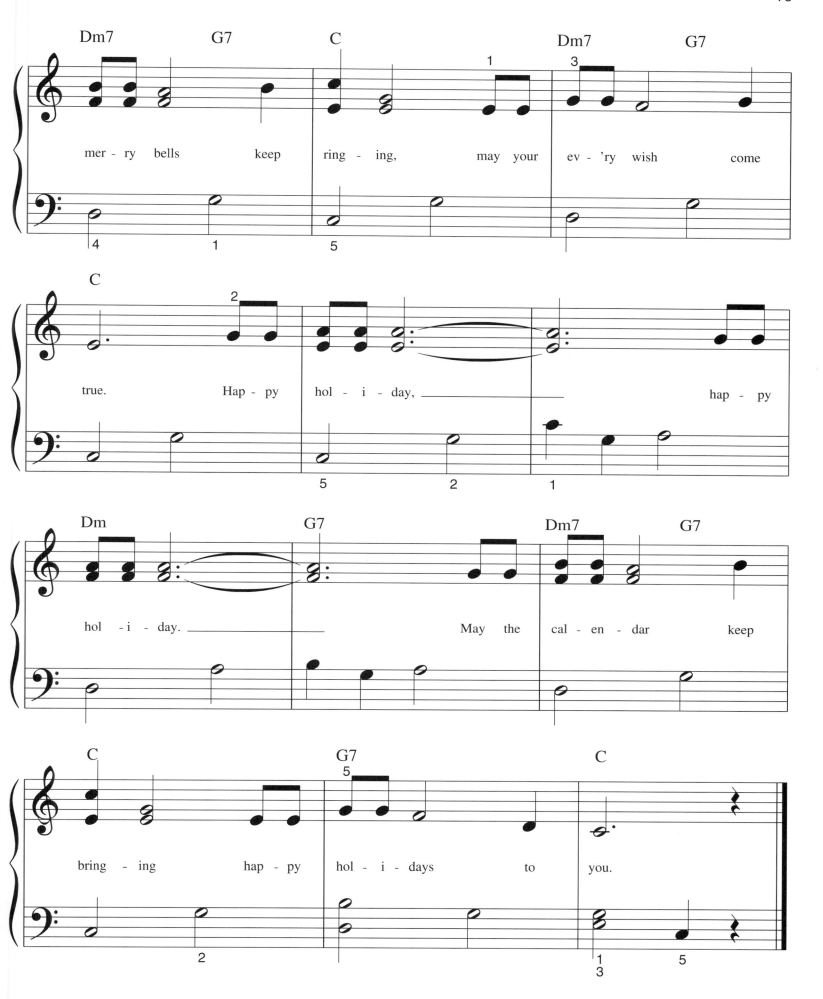

THE GIFT

Words and Music by TOM DOUGLAS
and JIM BRICKMAN

Win - ter snow is / fall - ing ___ down,
Watch - ing as you / soft - ly ___ sleep,

chil - dren laugh - ing / all a - round, / lights are / turn - ing on, ___
what I'd give if / I could ___ keep / just / this ___ mo -

- ment / like a / fair - y tale ___ come true.
if / on - ly time ___ stood still.

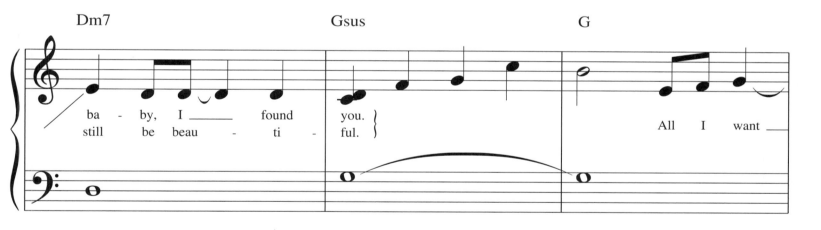

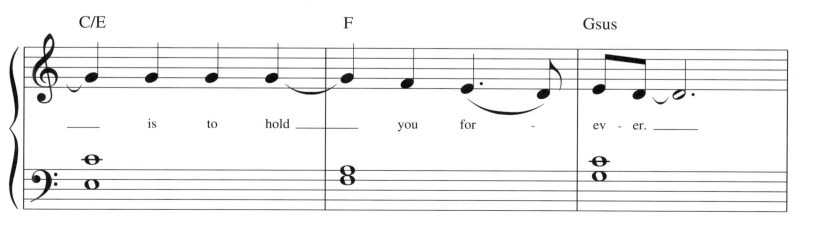

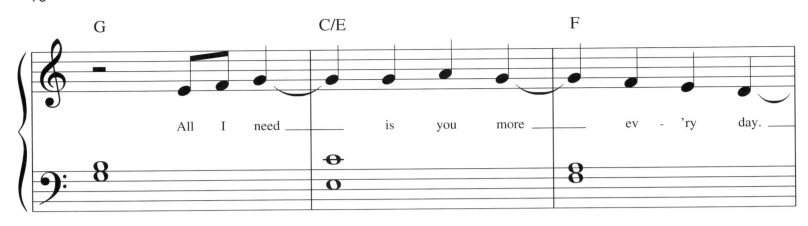

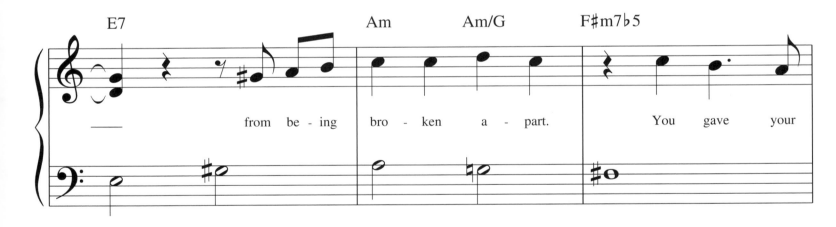

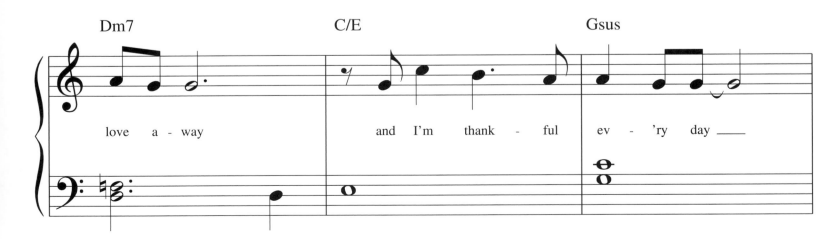

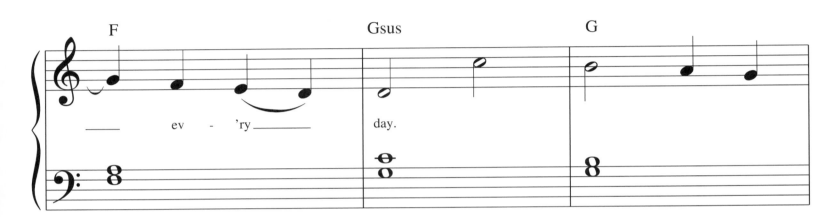

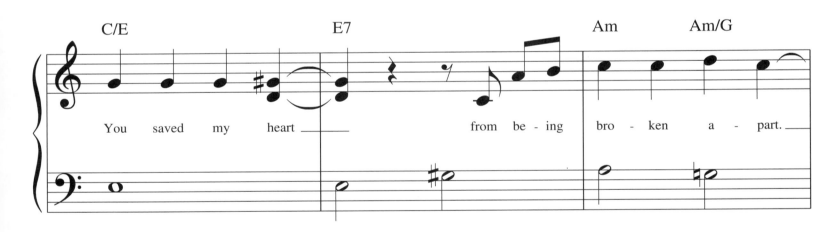

I can't find the words to say that I'm thank - ful _____

ev - 'ry day _____ for the gift.

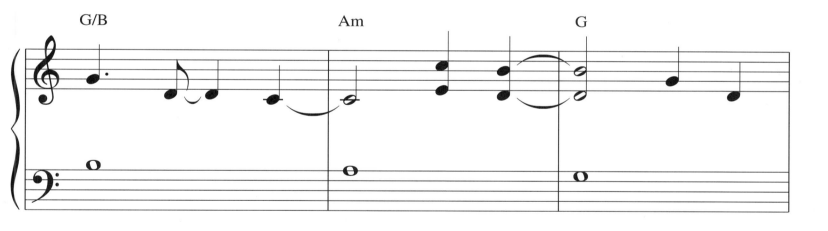

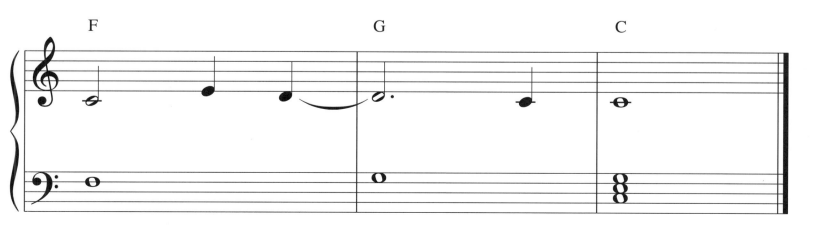

GO, TELL IT ON THE MOUNTAIN

African-American Spiritual
Verses by JOHN W. WORK, JR.

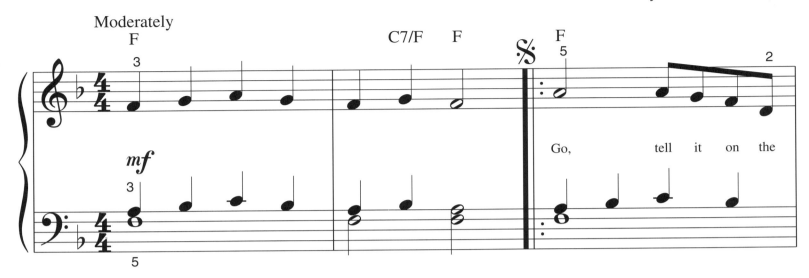

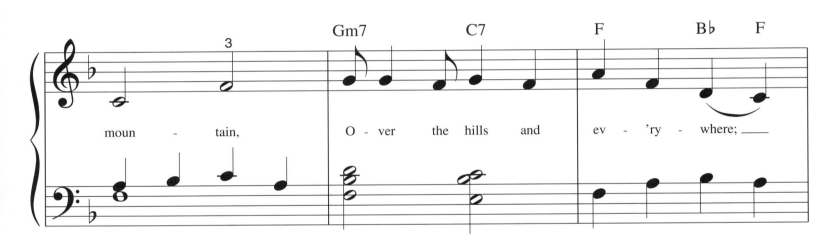

Gm7 C7 F B♭ F F
Fine
Je - sus Christ is born.
When I was a
He made me a
seek - er, I
watch - man up -
Gm7
sought both night and
on the cit - y
F
day; I asked the Lord to help me, And
wall; And if I am a Christ - ian, I
G7
He showed me the
am the least of
1. C7
way.
2. C7
D.S. al Fine
all.

GOOD CHRISTIAN MEN, REJOICE

14th Century Latin Text
Translated by JOHN MASON NEALE
14th Century German Melody

Good Chris - tian men re - joice with heart and soul and voice, Give ye heed to what we say:

Chris - tian men re - joice with heart and soul and voice, Now ye hear of end - less bliss:

GOOD KING WENCESLAS

Words by JOHN M. NEALE
Music from *Piae Cantiones*

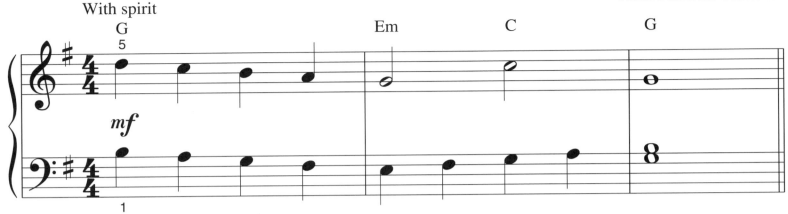

With spirit

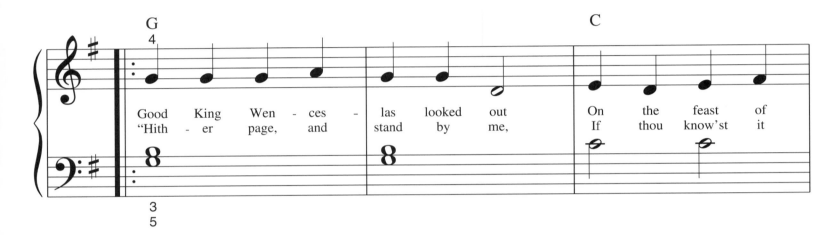

Good King Wen - ces - las looked out
"Hith - er page, and stand by me,

On the feast of
If thou know'st it

Steph - en,
tell - ing,

When the snow lay
Yon - der peas - ant,

round a - bout,
who is he?

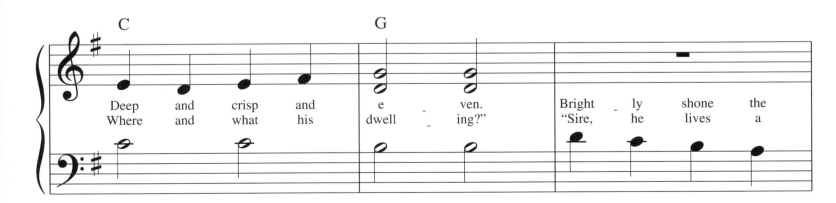

Deep and crisp and
Where and what his

e - ven.
dwell - ing?"

Bright - ly shone the
"Sire, he lives a

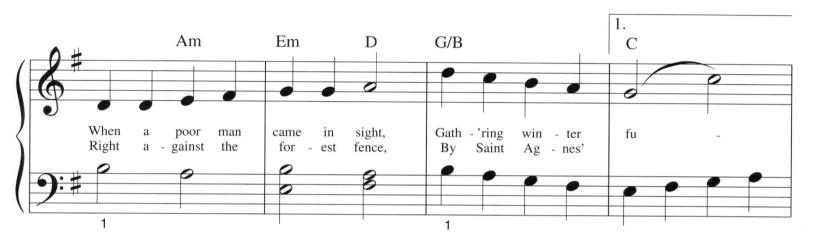

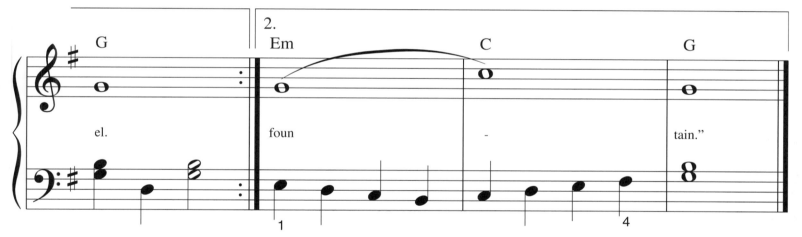

3. "Bring me flesh, and bring me wine,
   Bring me pine-logs hither;
   Thou and I will see him dine,
   When we bear them thither."
   Page and monarch forth they went,
   Forth they went together;
   Through the rude winds wild lament
   And the bitter weather.

4. "Sire, the night is darker now,
   And the wind blows stronger;
   Fails my heart, I know not how,
   I can go no longer."
   "Mark my footsteps, my good page,
   Tread thou in them boldly;
   Thou shall find the winter's rage
   Frees they blood less coldly."

5. In his master's steps he trod,
   Where the snow lay dinted;
   Heat was in the very sod
   Which the saint had printed
   Therefore, Christian men, be sure,
   Wealth or rank possessing,
   Ye who now will bless the poor,
   Shall yourselves find blessing.

THE GREATEST GIFT OF ALL

Words and Music by
JOHN JARVIS

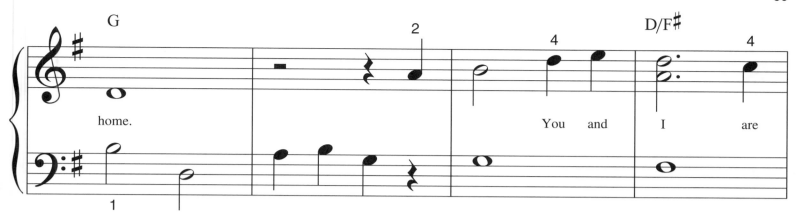

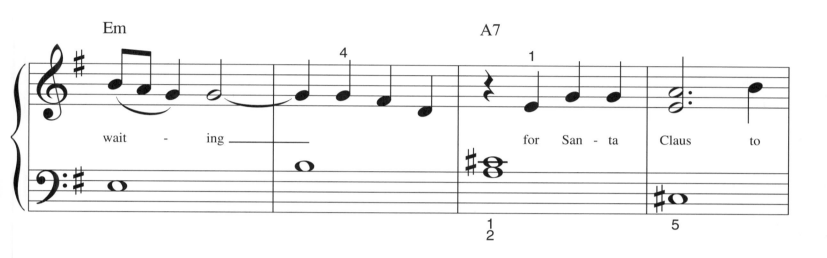

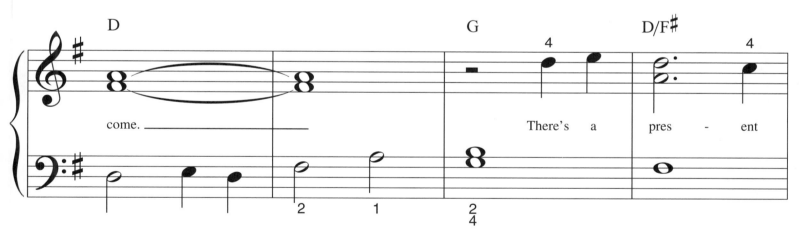

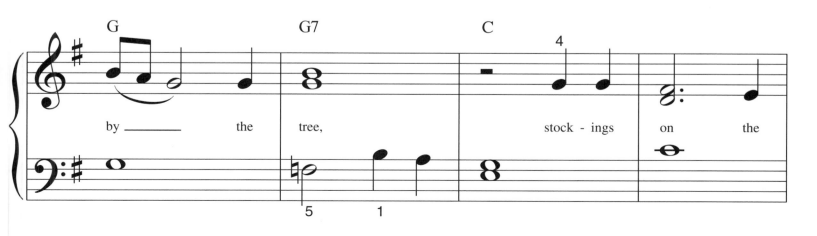

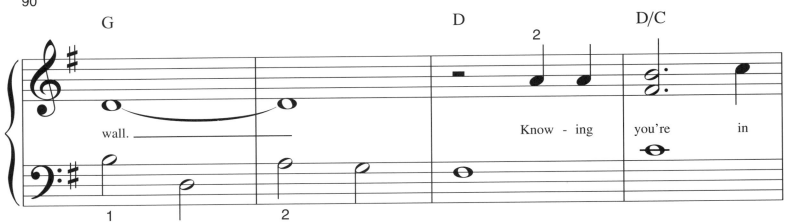

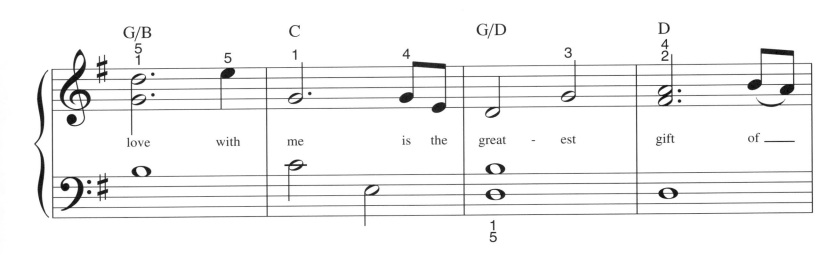

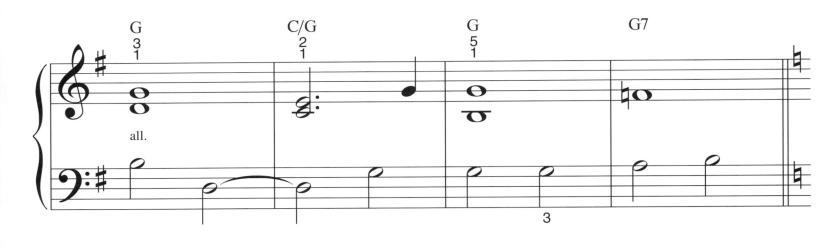

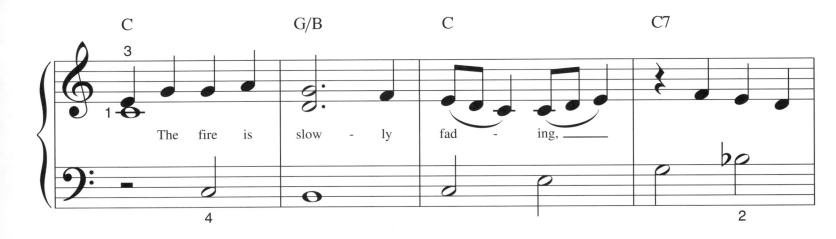

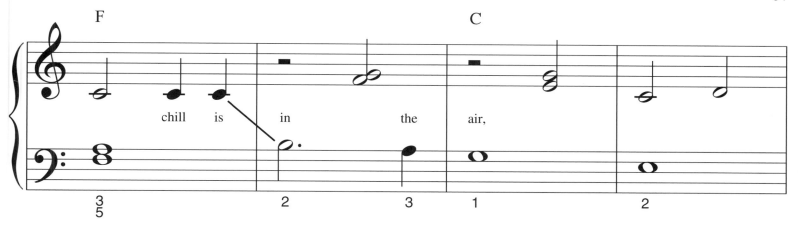

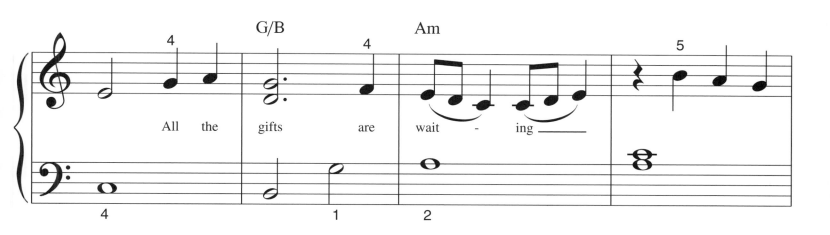

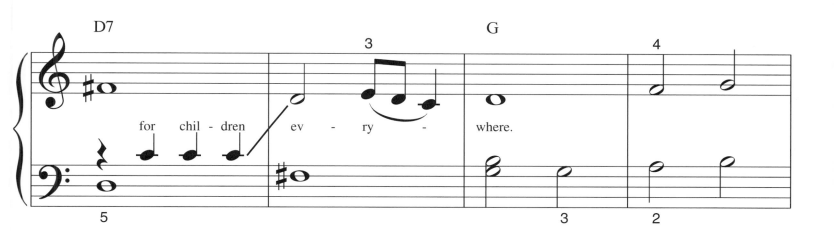

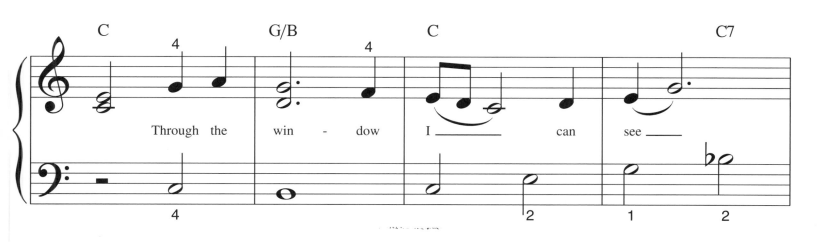

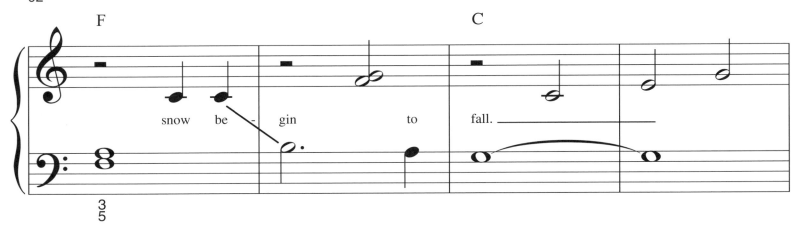

snow be - gin to fall. _____

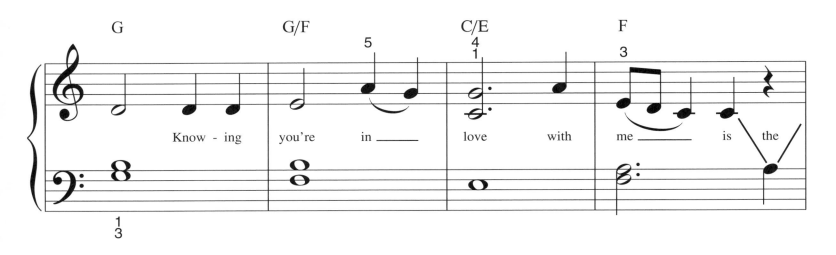

Know - ing you're in _____ love with me _____ is the

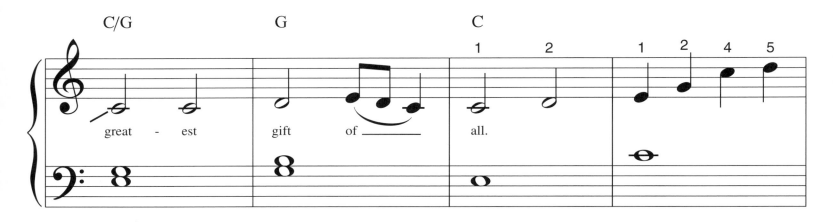

great - est gift of _____ all.

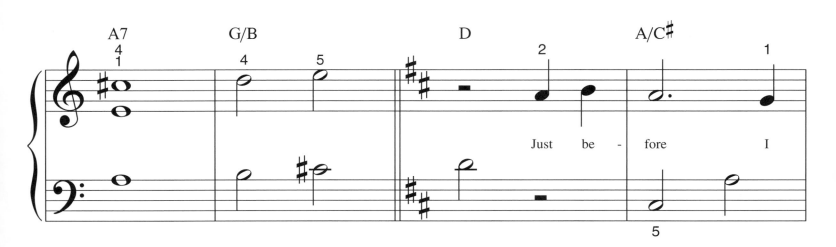

Just be - fore I

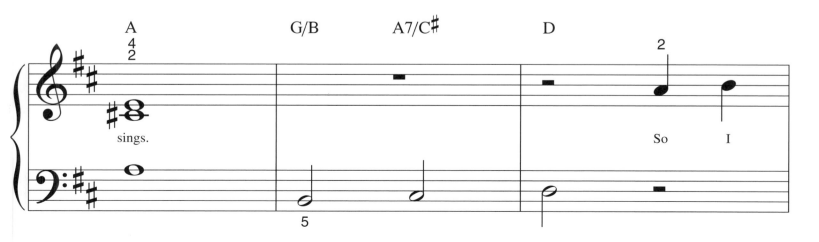

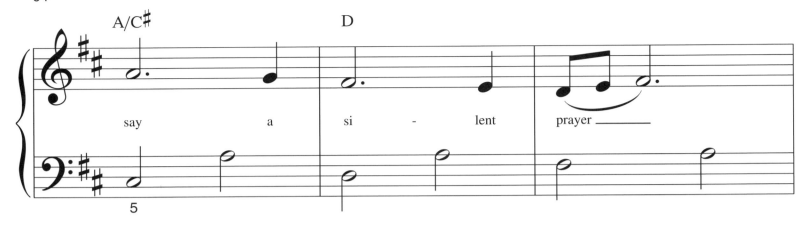

say   a   si -   lent   prayer ____

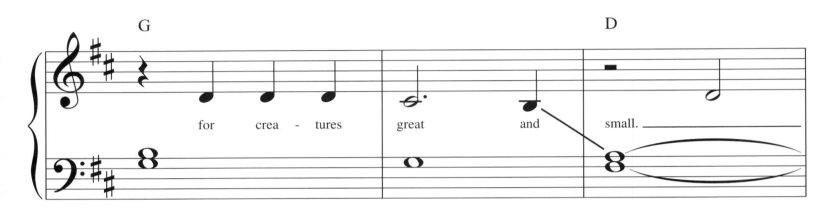

for   crea - tures   great   and   small. ____

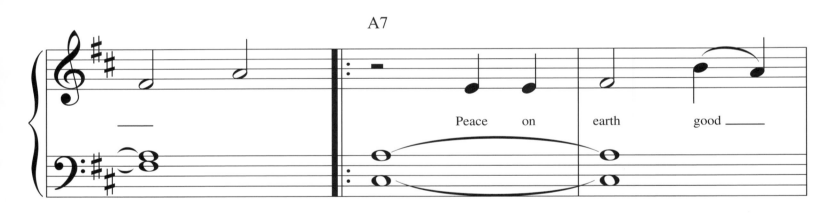

____   Peace   on   earth   good ____

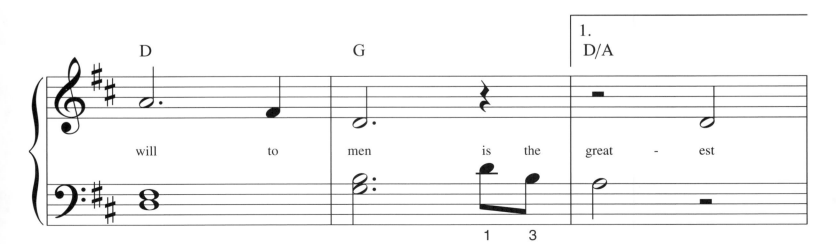

will   to   men   is   the   great -   est

HAPPY XMAS
(War Is Over)

Words and Music by JOHN LENNON
and YOKO ONO

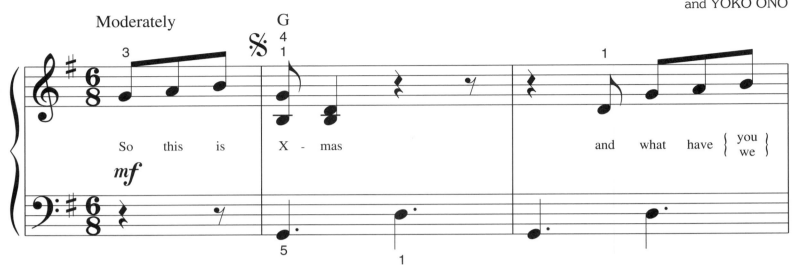

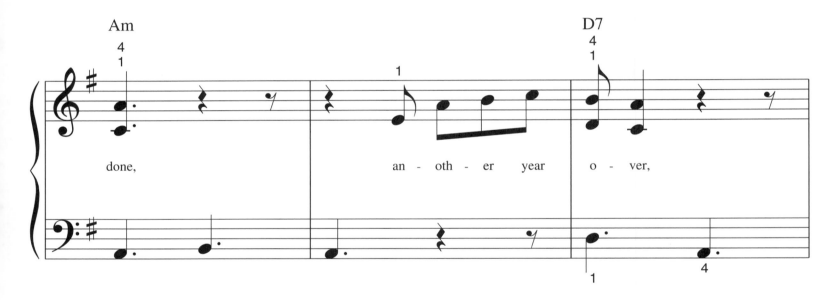

98

A HOLLY JOLLY CHRISTMAS

Music and Lyrics by
JOHNNY MARKS

Moderately Bright

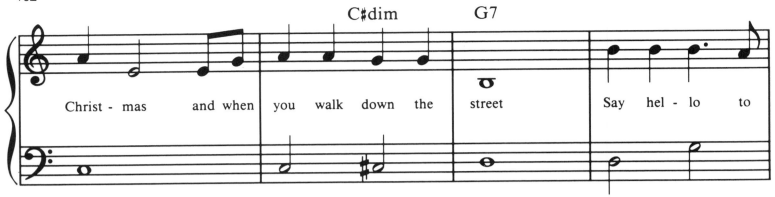

Christ - mas and when you walk down the street Say hel - lo to

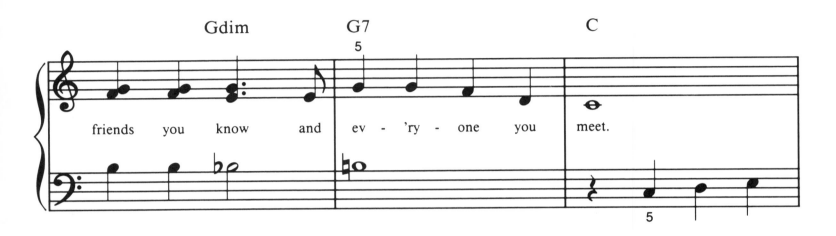

friends you know and ev - 'ry - one you meet.

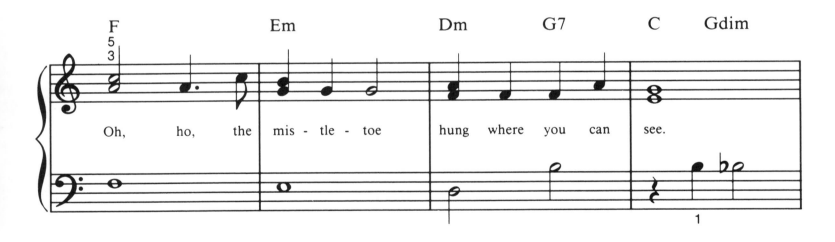

Oh, ho, the mis - tle - toe hung where you can see.

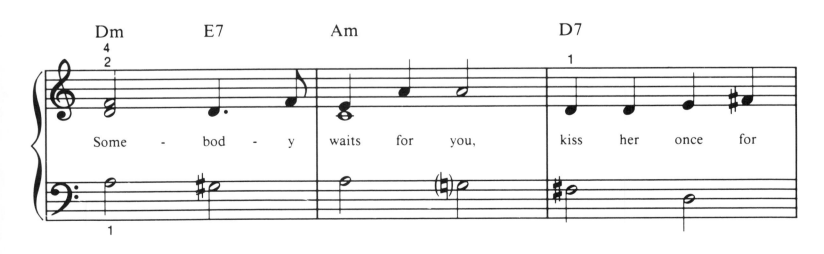

Some - bod - y waits for you, kiss her once for

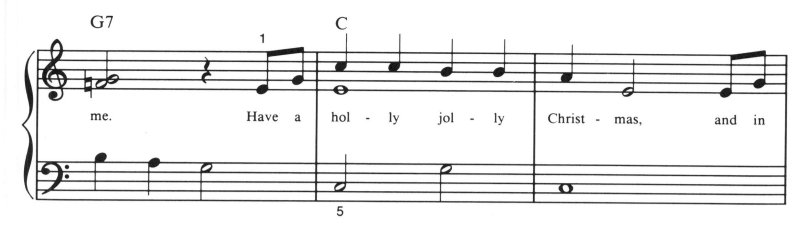

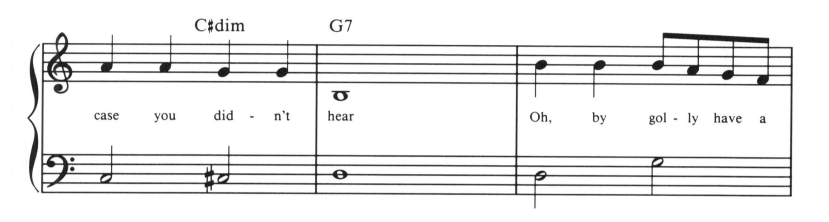

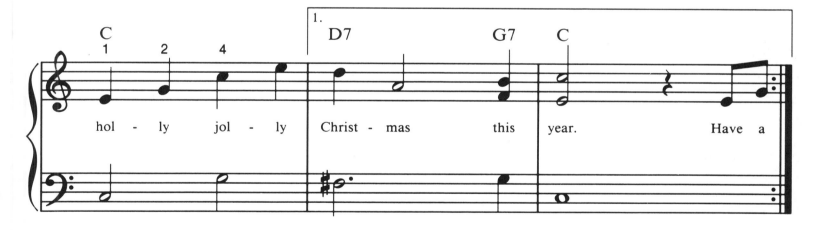

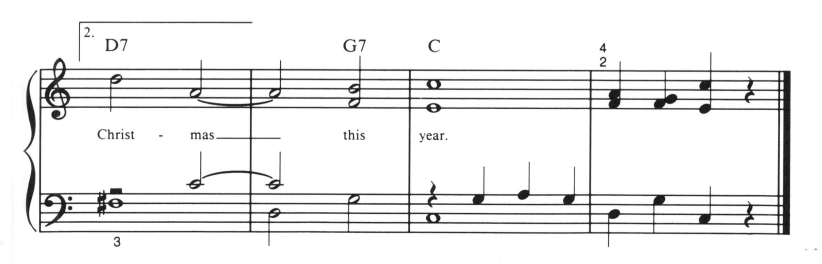

HARK! THE HERALD ANGELS SING

Words by CHARLES WESLEY
Altered by GEORGE WHITEFIELD
Music by FELIX MENDELSSOHN-BARTHOLDY
Arranged by WILLIAM H. CUMMINGS

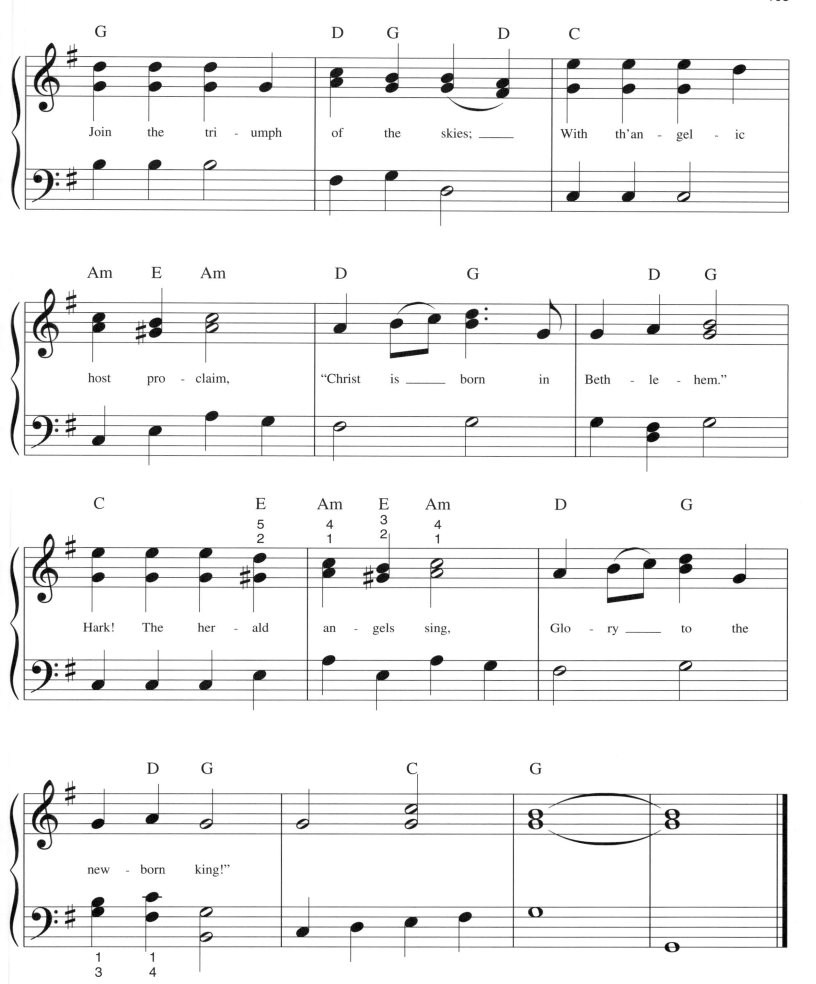

I HEARD THE BELLS ON CHRISTMAS DAY

Words by HENRY WADSWORTH LONGFELLOW
Adapted by JOHNNY MARKS
Music by JOHNNY MARKS

I SAW MOMMY KISSING SANTA CLAUS

Words and Music by
TOMMIE CONNOR

I WONDER AS I WANDER

By JOHN JACOB NILES

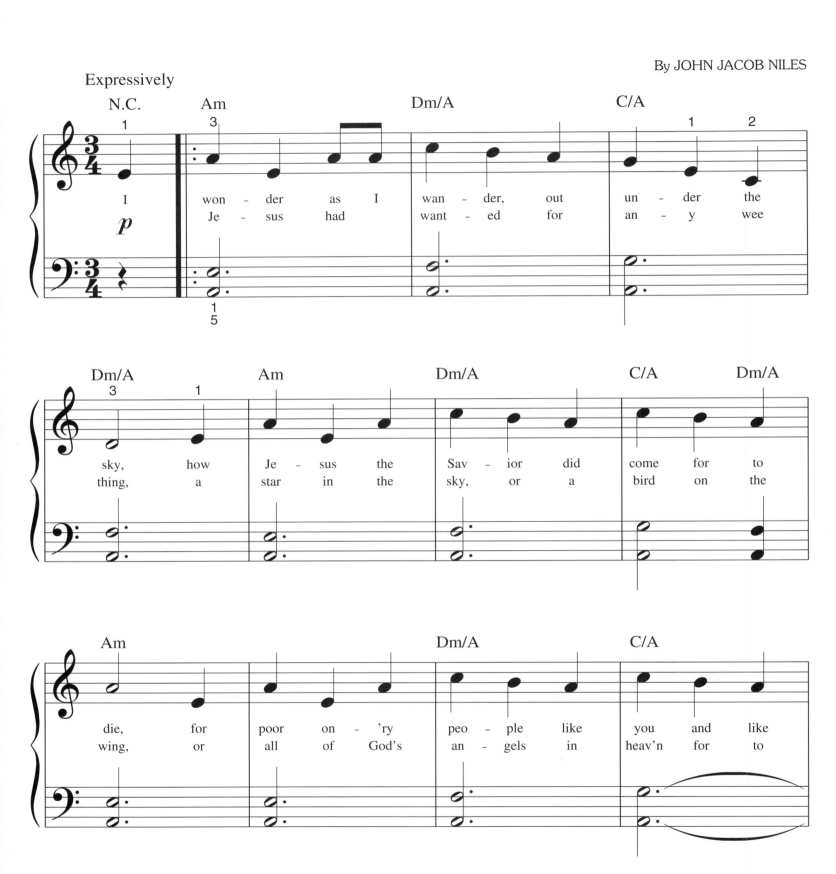

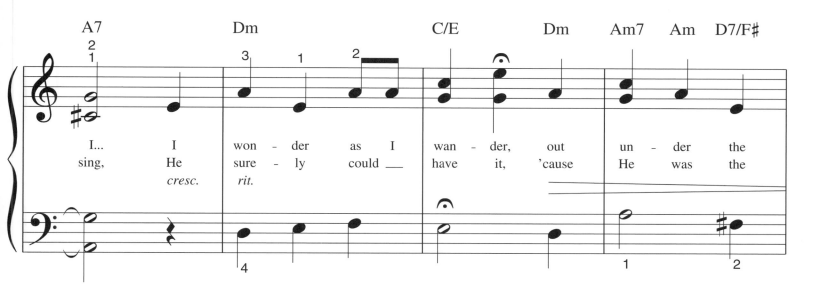

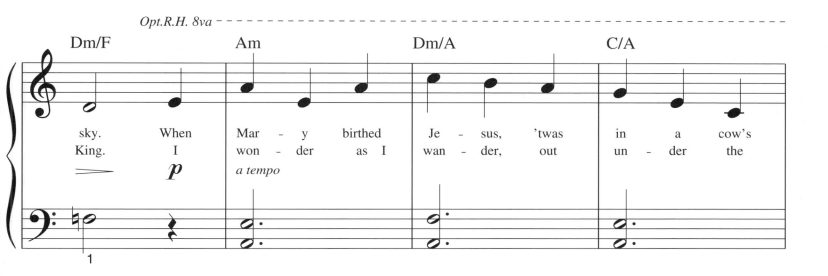

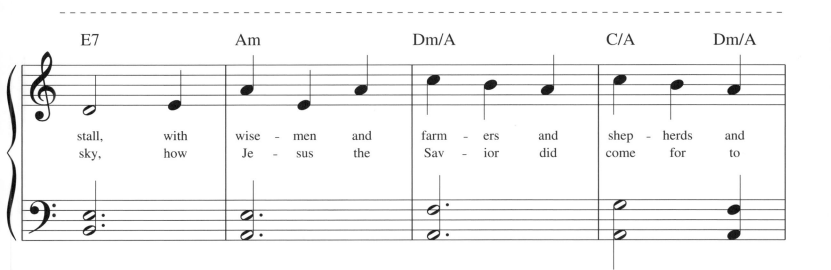

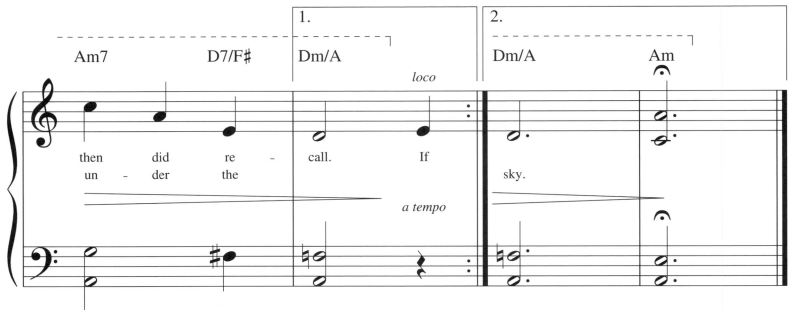

I'LL BE HOME FOR CHRISTMAS

Words and Music by KIM GANNON
and WALTER KENT

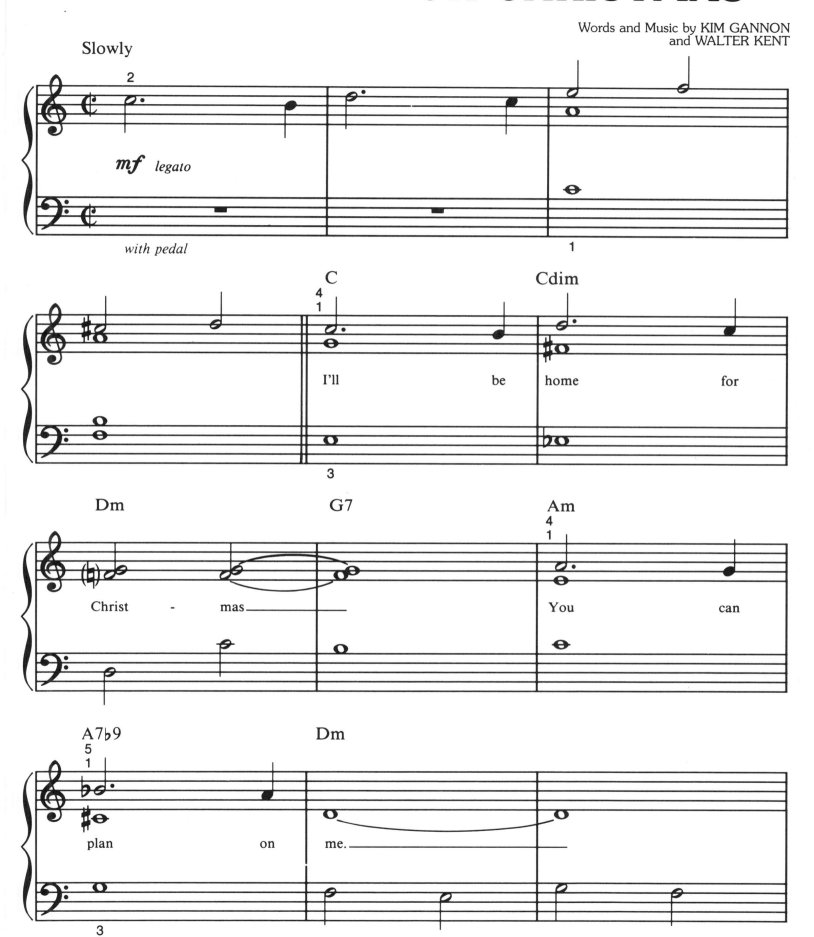

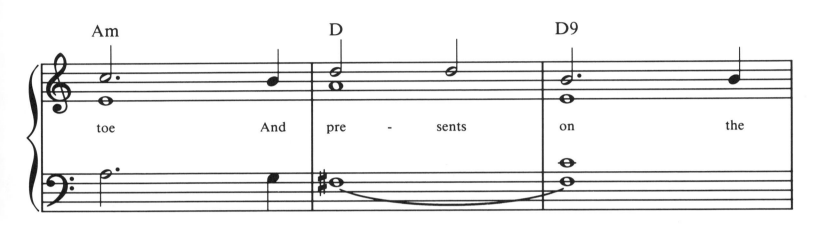

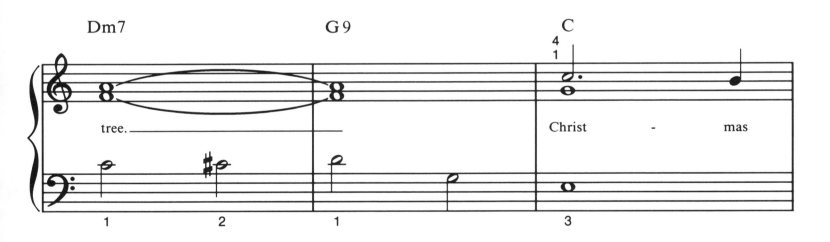

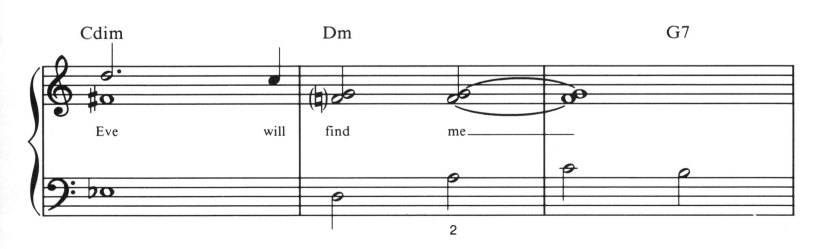

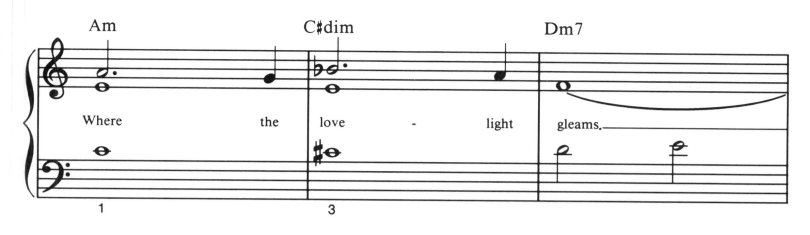

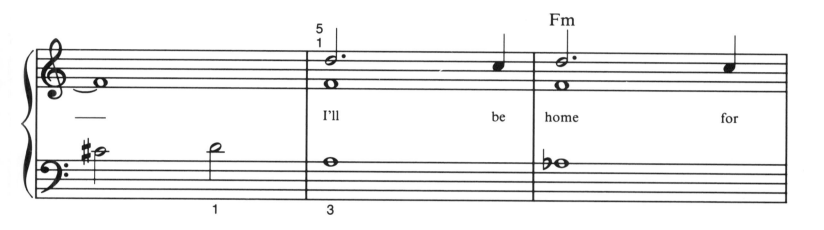

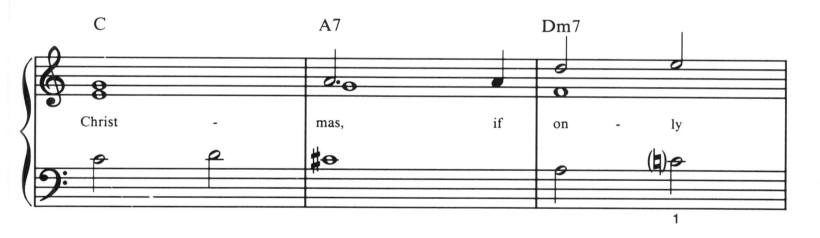

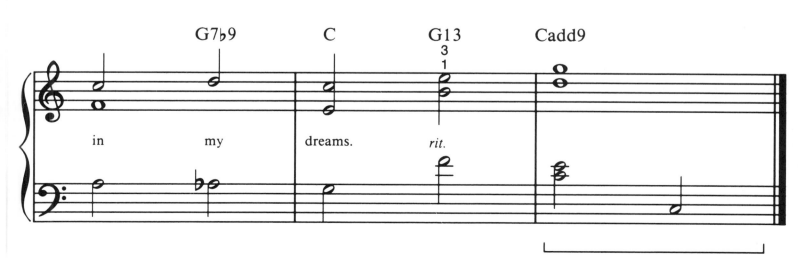

IT CAME UPON THE MIDNIGHT CLEAR

Words by EDMUND HAMILTON SEARS
Music by RICHARD STORRS WILLIS

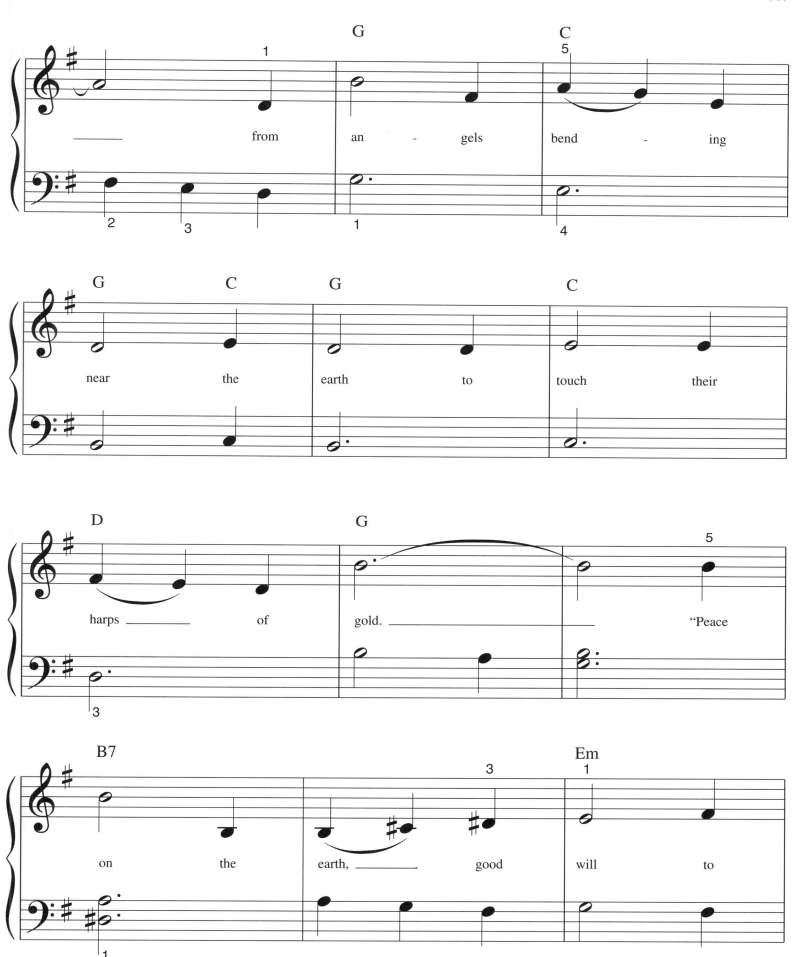

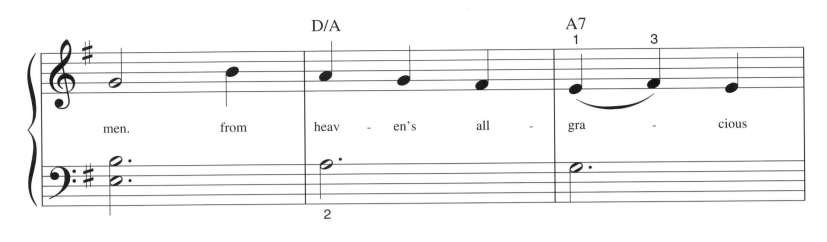

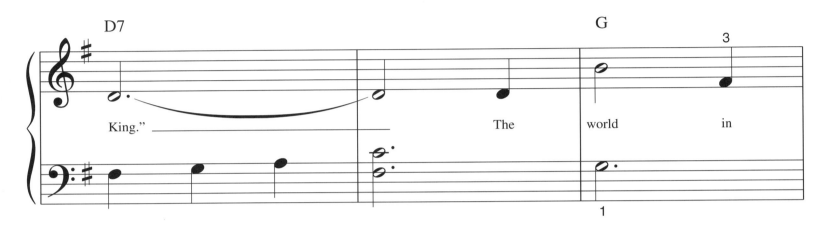

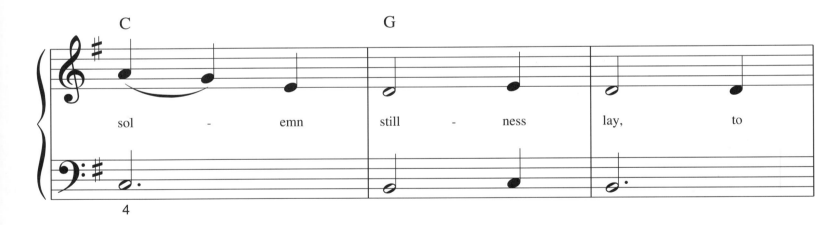

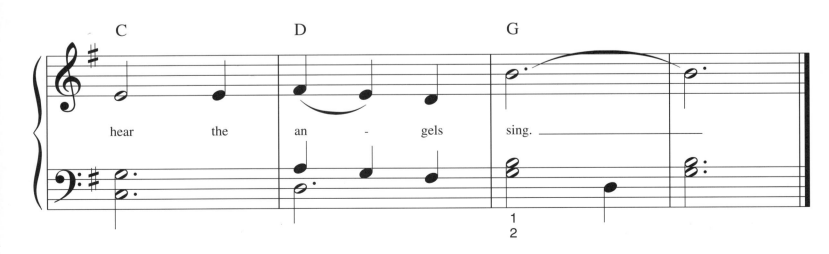

IT'S BEGINNING TO LOOK LIKE CHRISTMAS

By MEREDITH WILLSON

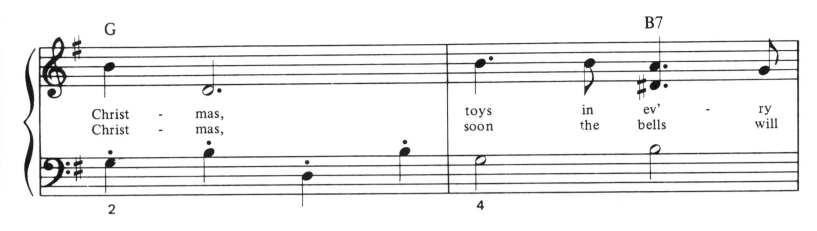

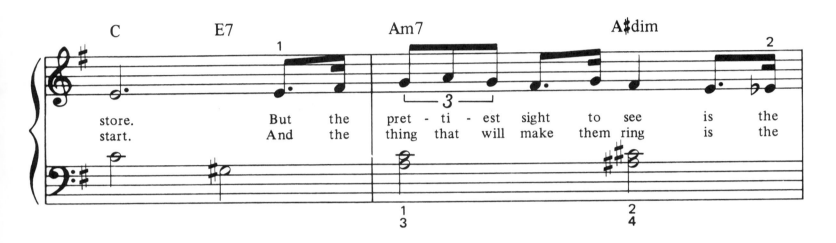

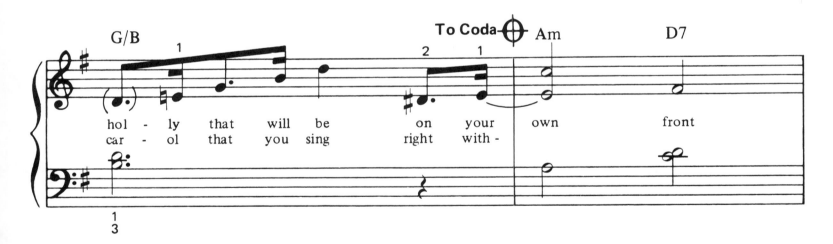

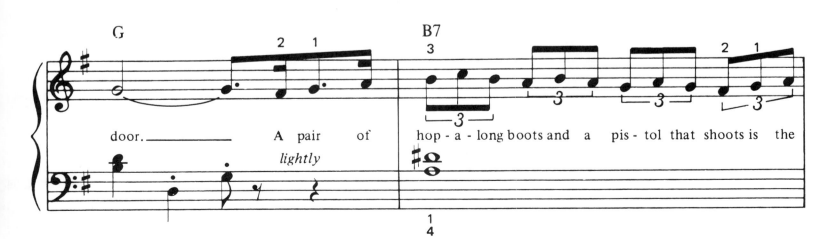

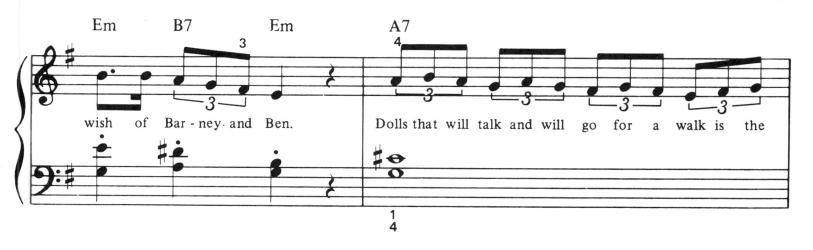

wish of Bar - ney and Ben. Dolls that will talk and will go for a walk is the

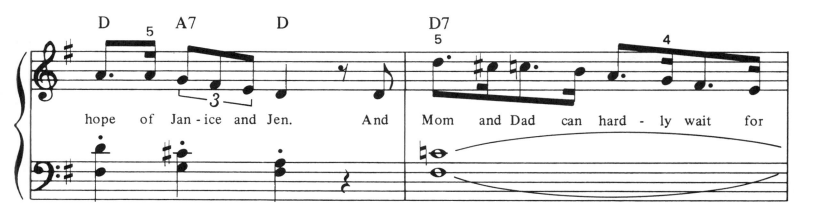

hope of Jan - ice and Jen. And Mom and Dad can hard - ly wait for

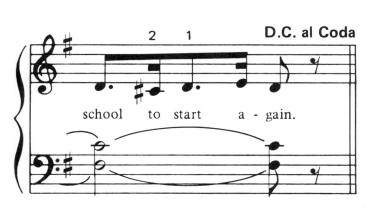

school to start a - gain.

D.C. al Coda

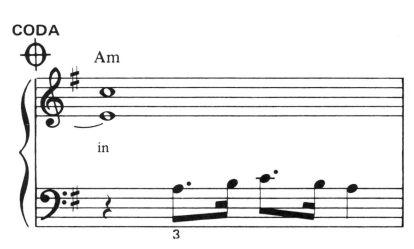

CODA

Am

in

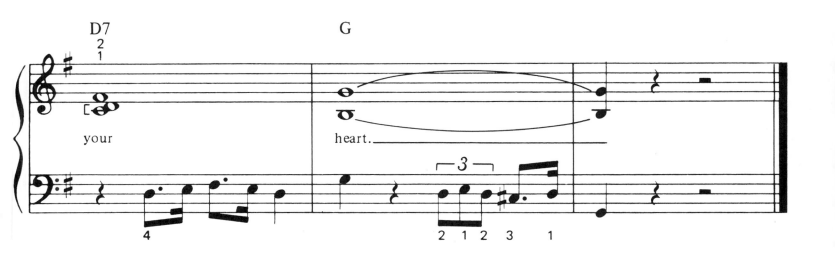

your heart.

JINGLE-BELL ROCK

Words and Music by JOE BEAL
and JIM BOOTHE

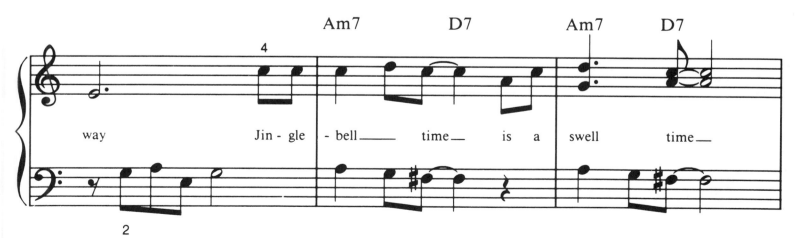

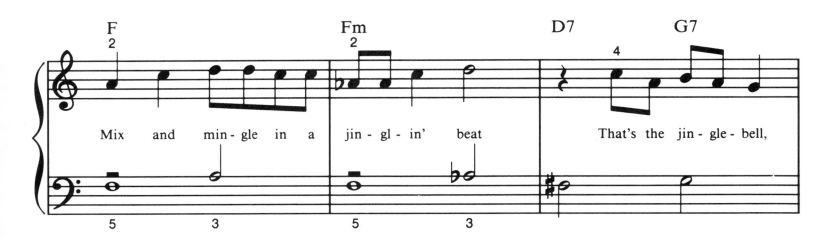

JINGLE BELLS

Words and Music by
J. PIERPONT

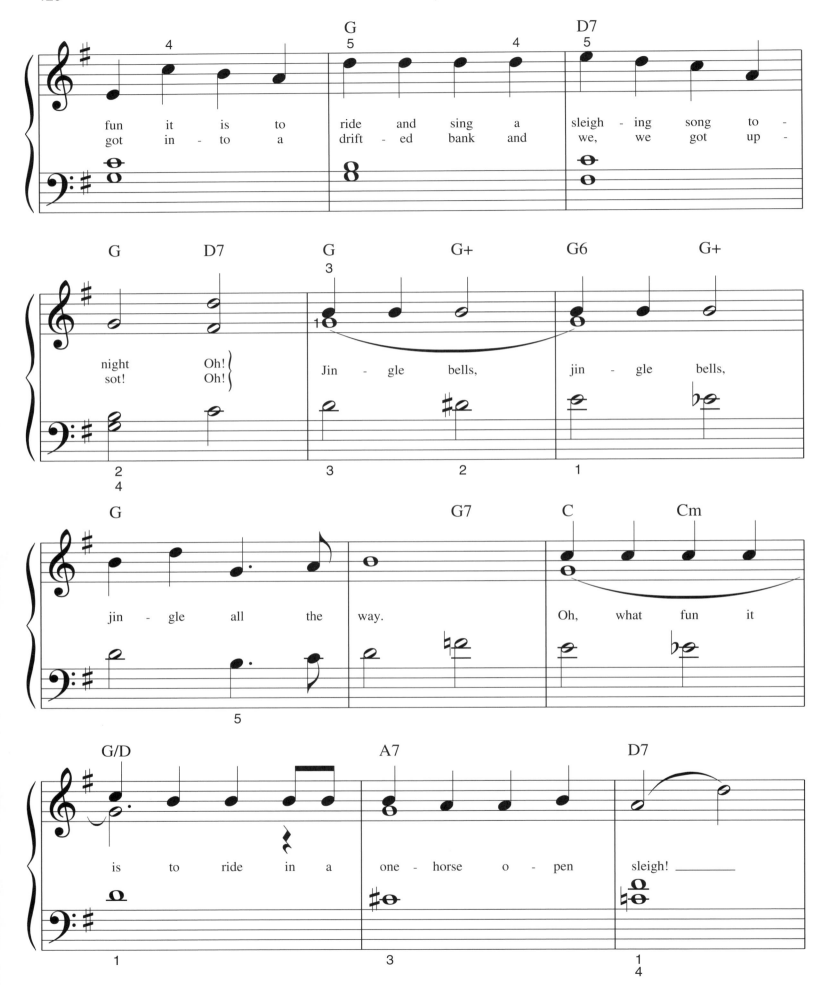

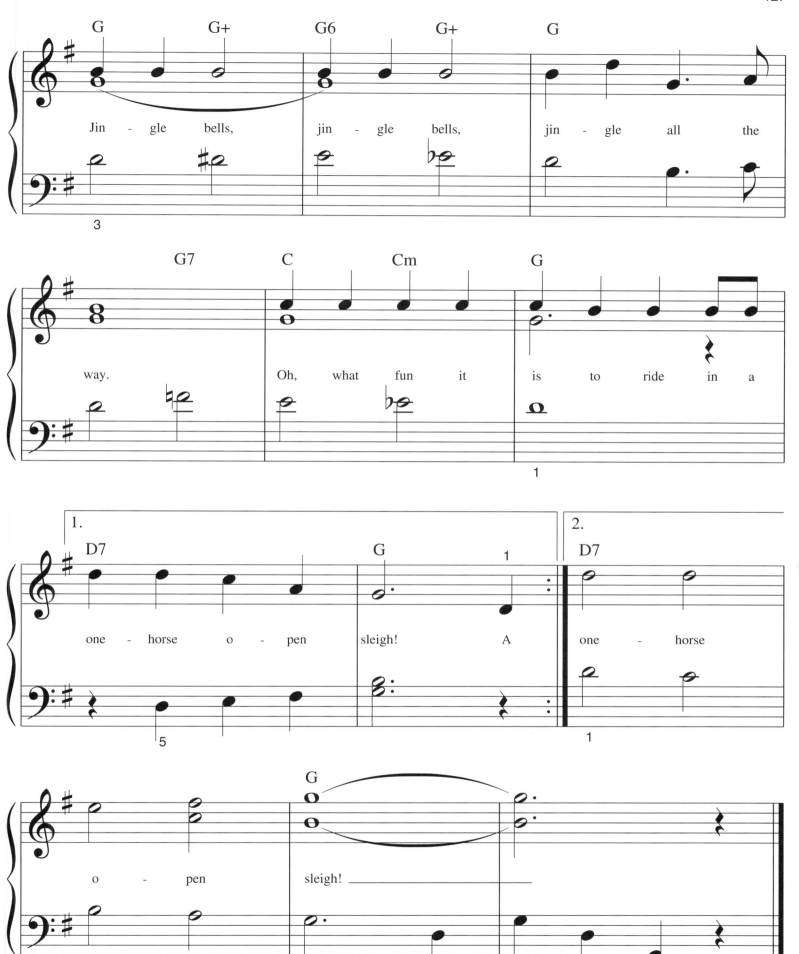

JOY TO THE WORLD

Words by ISAAC WATTS
Music by GEORGE FRIDERIC HANDEL
Arranged by LOWELL MASON

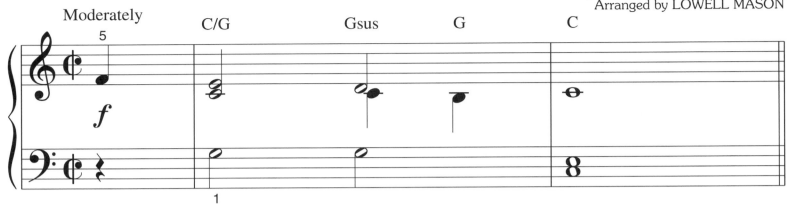

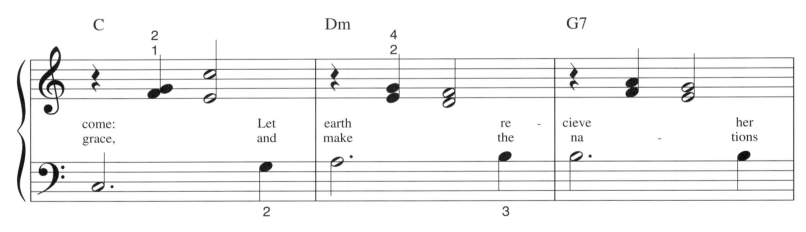

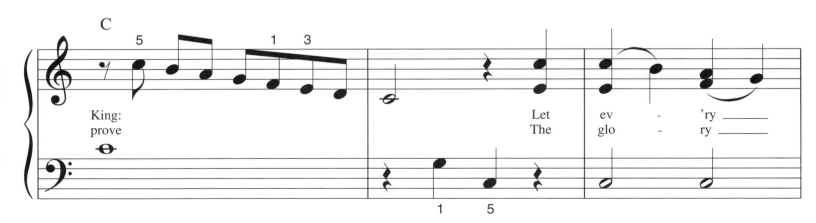

LAST CHRISTMAS

Words and Music by
GEORGE MICHAEL

133

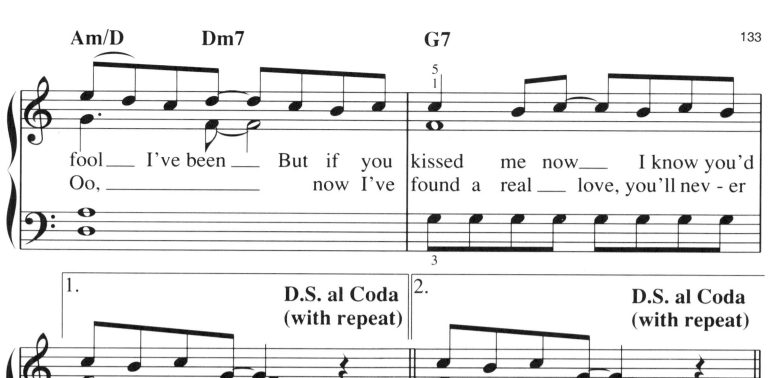

Am/D   Dm7   G7

fool ___ I've been ___ But if you | kissed   me now___   I know you'd
Oo, _____   now I've | found a   real ___ love, you'll nev - er

1.   **D.S. al Coda (with repeat)** **2.**   **D.S. al Coda (with repeat)**

fool me a - gain.___   fool me a - gain. ___

CODA

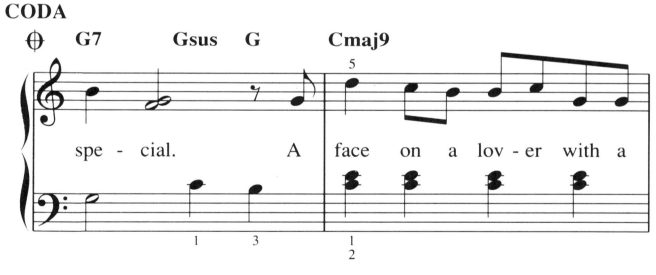

G7   Gsus   G   Cmaj9

spe - cial.   A | face   on a lov - er with a

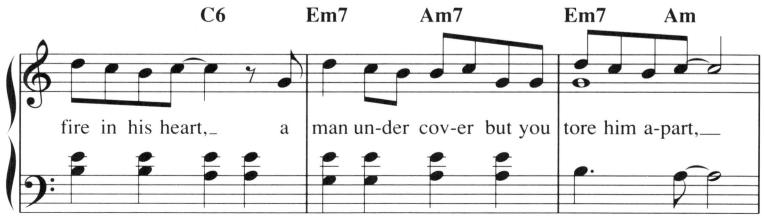

C6   Em7   Am7   Em7   Am

fire in his heart,_   a | man un-der cov-er but you | tore him a-part,___

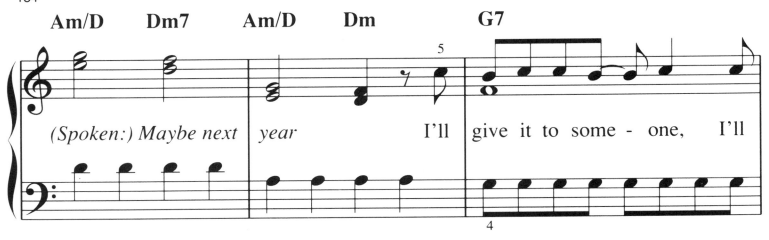

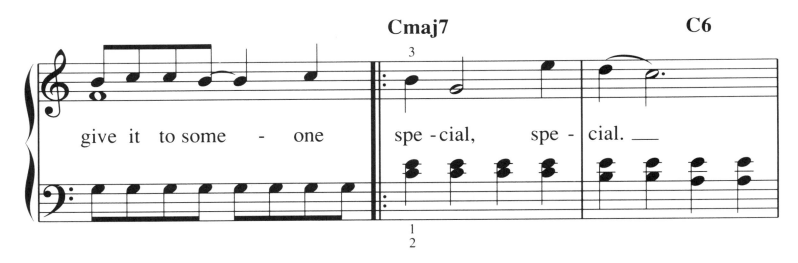

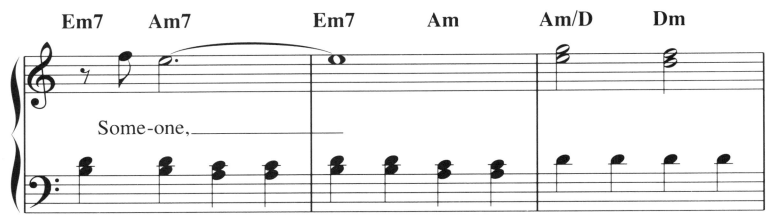

LET IT SNOW! LET IT SNOW! LET IT SNOW!

Words by SAMMY CAHN
Music by JULE STYNE

Moderately

Oh the weath-er out-side is fright-ful But the fire is so de-light-ful, And since we've no place to go, Let it snow! Let it snow! Let it snow! It

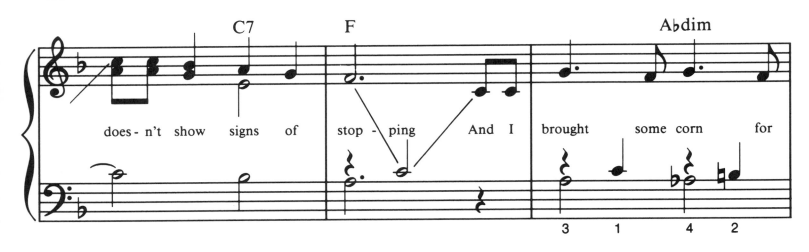

doesn't show signs of stop-ping And I brought some corn for

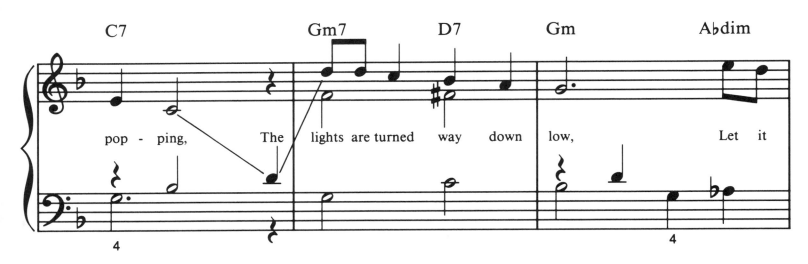

pop-ping, The lights are turned way down low, Let it

snow! Let it snow! Let it snow! When we fin-al-ly kiss good-

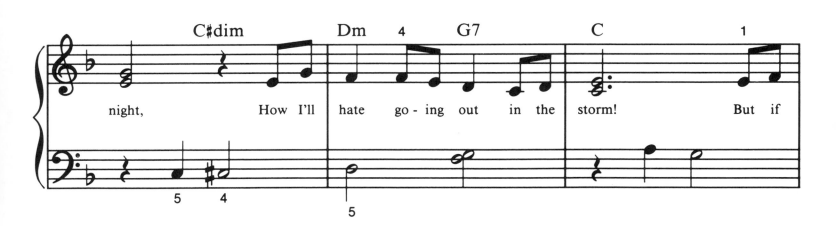

night, How I'll hate go-ing out in the storm! But if

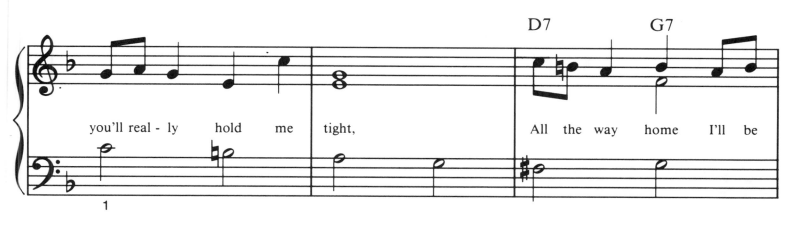

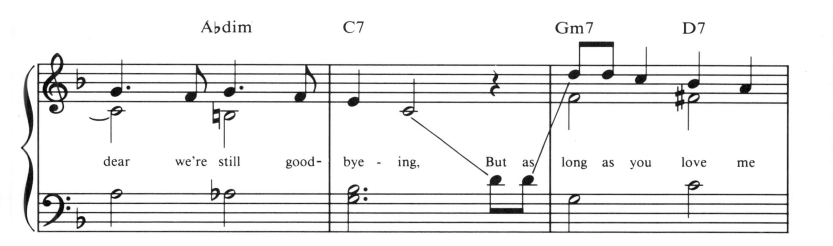

MERRY CHRISTMAS, DARLING

Words and Music by RICHARD CARPENTER
and FRANK POOLER

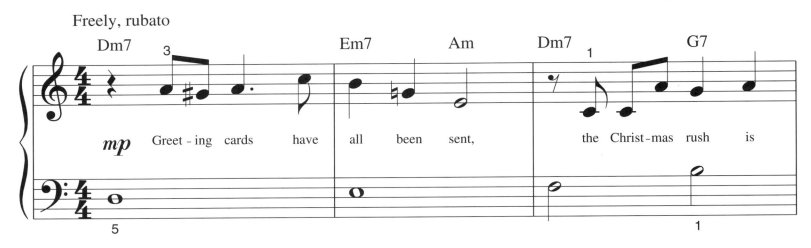

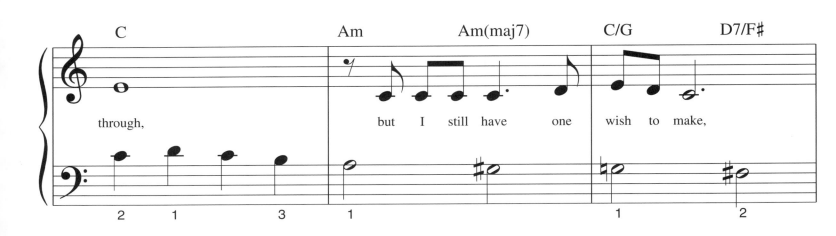

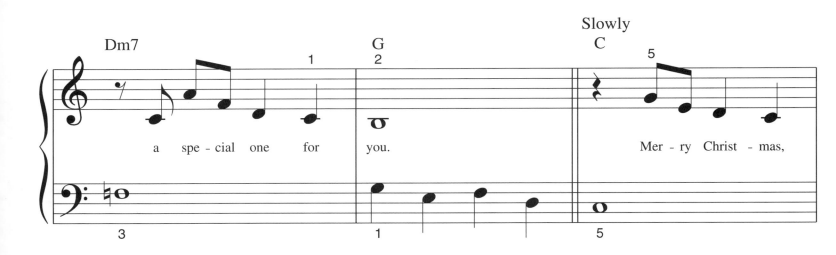

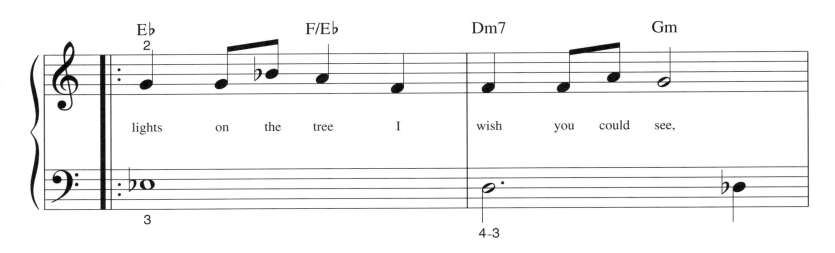

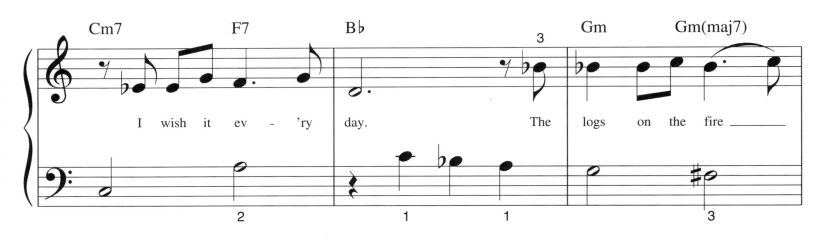

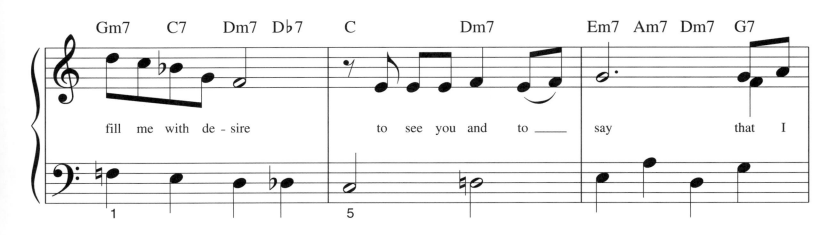

MISTER SANTA

Words and Music by
PAT BALLARD

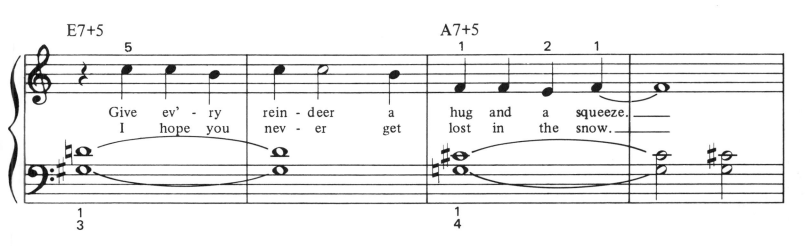

O COME, ALL YE FAITHFUL
(Adeste Fideles)

Words and Music by JOHN FRANCIS WADE
Latin Words translated by FREDERICK OAKELEY

O HOLY NIGHT

French Words by PLACIDE CAPPEAU
English Words by JOHN S. DWIGHT
Music by ADOLPHE ADAM

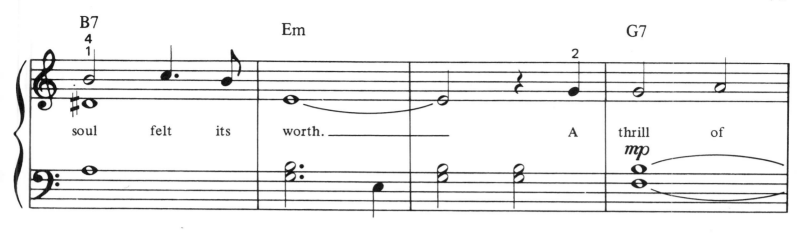

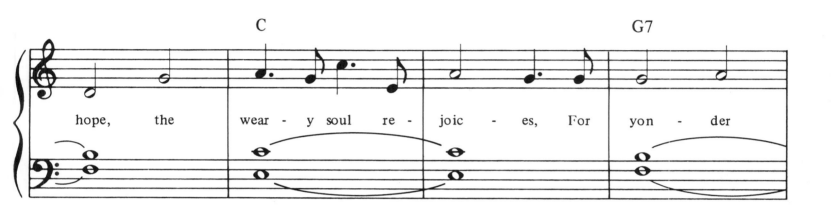

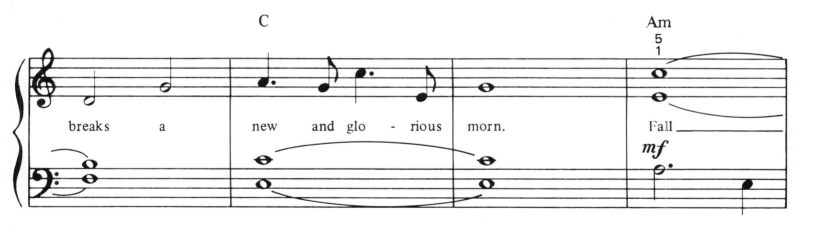

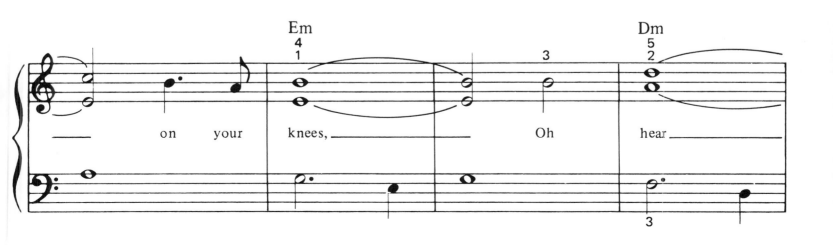

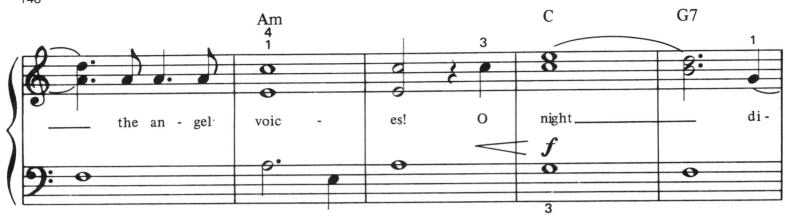

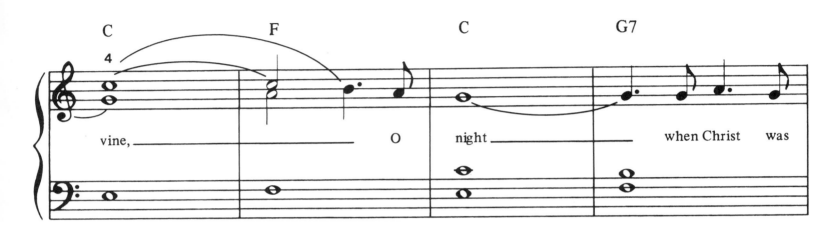

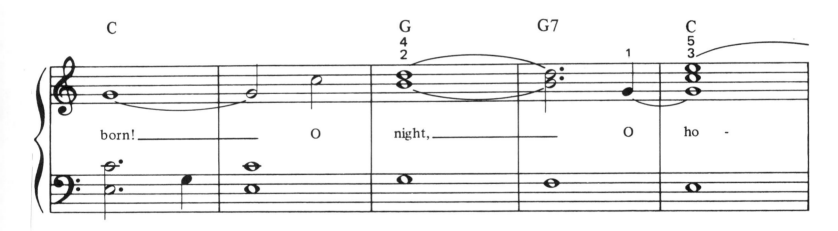

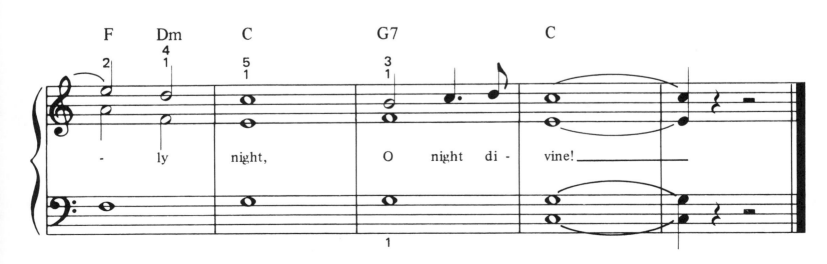

O LITTLE TOWN OF BETHLEHEM

Words by PHILLIPS BROOKS
Music by LEWIS H. REDNER

PLEASE COME HOME FOR CHRISTMAS

Words and Music by CHARLES BROWN
and GENE REDD

ROCKIN' AROUND THE CHRISTMAS TREE

Music and Lyrics by
JOHNNY MARKS

RUDOLPH THE RED-NOSED REINDEER

Music and Lyrics by
JOHNNY MARKS

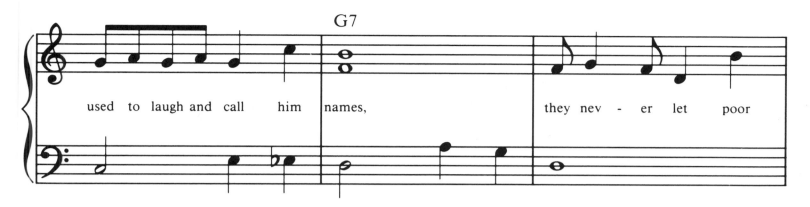

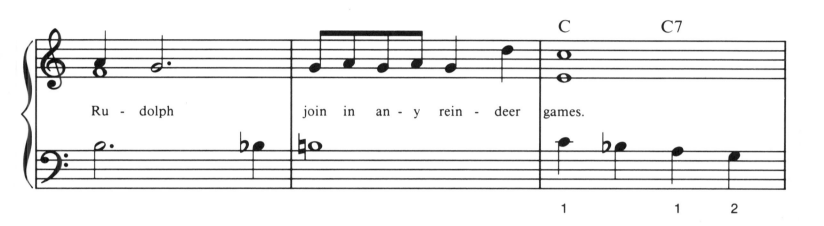

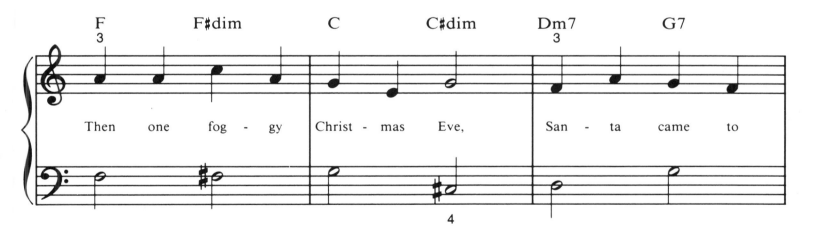

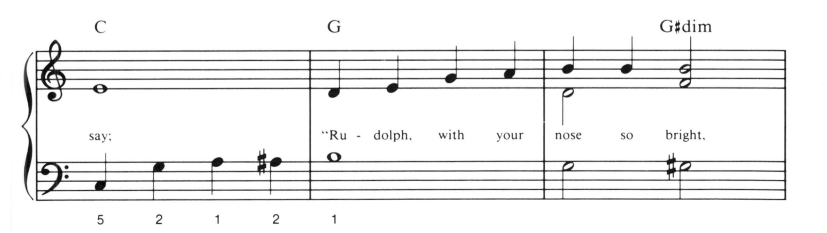

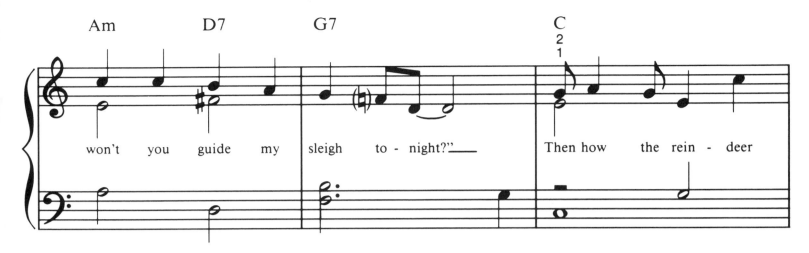

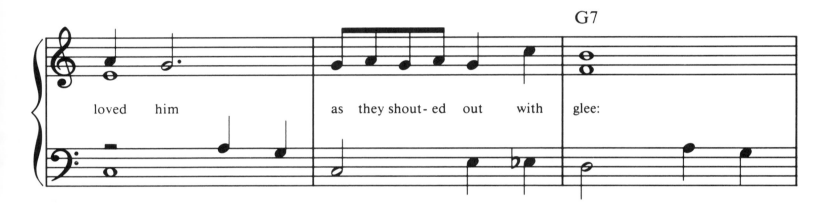

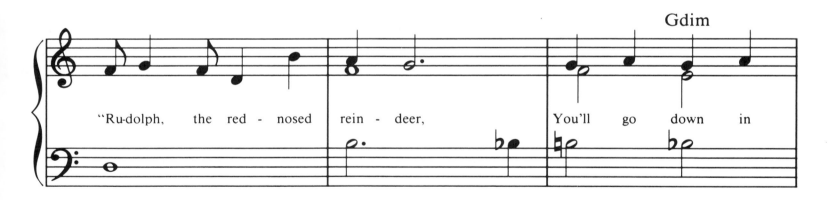

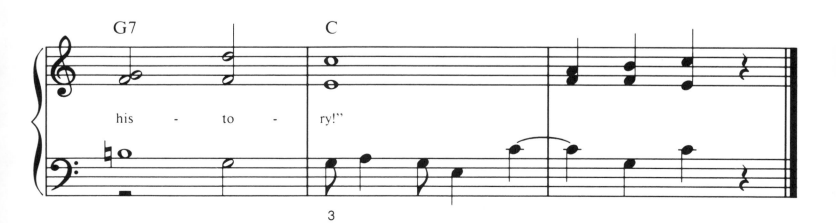

3

SILVER BELLS
from the Paramount Picture THE LEMON DROP KID

Words and Music by JAY LIVINGSTON
and RAY EVANS

Cit - y side - walks, bus - y side - walks dressed in
street lights, ev - en stop lights blink a

hol - i - day style, In the air there's a
bright red and green, As the shop - pers rush

feel - ing of Christ - mas. Chil - dren
home with their treas - ures. Hear the

SILENT NIGHT

Words by JOSEPH MOHR
Translated by JOHN F. YOUNG
Music by FRANZ X. GRUBER

SOME CHILDREN SEE HIM

Lyric by WIHLA HUTSON
Music by ALFRED BURT

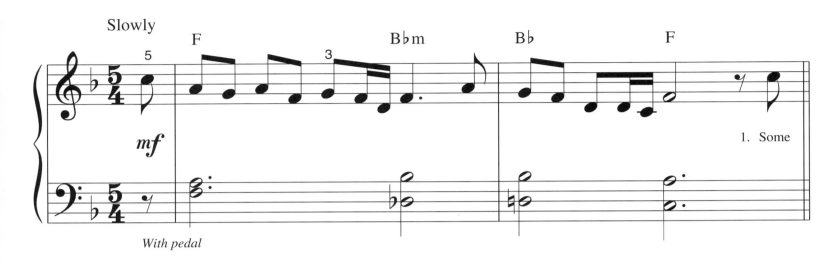

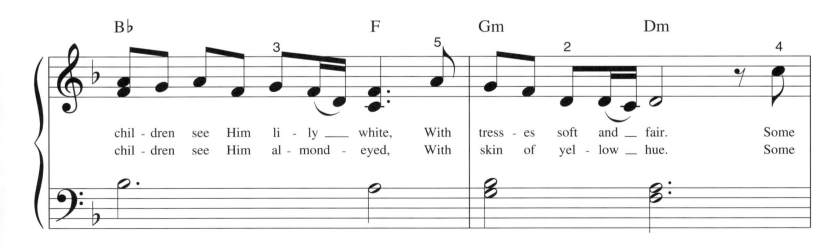

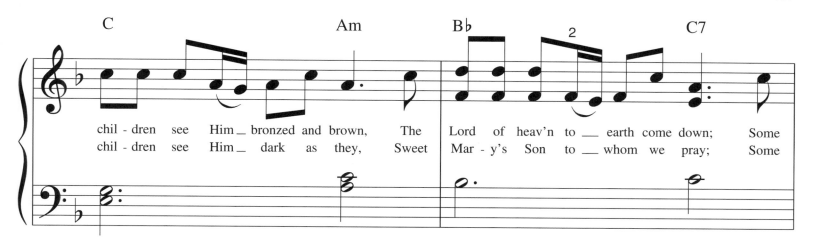

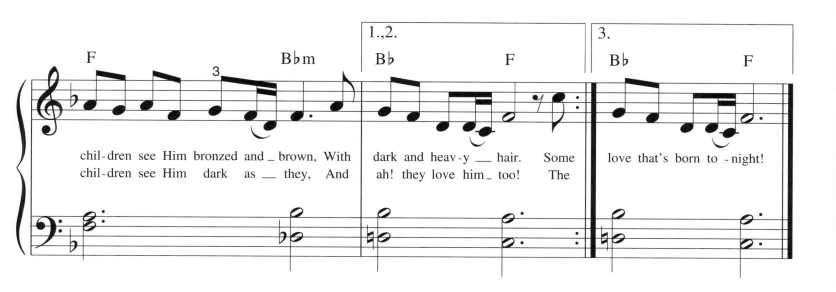

Additional Lyrics

3. The children in each diff'rent place
   Will see the Baby Jesus' face
   Like theirs, but bright with heav'nly grace,
   And filled with holy light.

   O lay aside each earthly thing,
   And with thy heart as offering,
   Come worship now the Infant King,
   'Tis love that's born tonight!

THE STAR CAROL

Lyric by WIHLA HUTSON
Music by ALFRED BURT

WE NEED A LITTLE CHRISTMAS

from MAME

Music and Lyric by
JERRY HERMAN

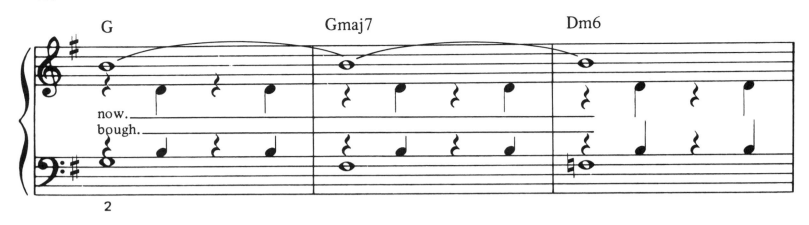

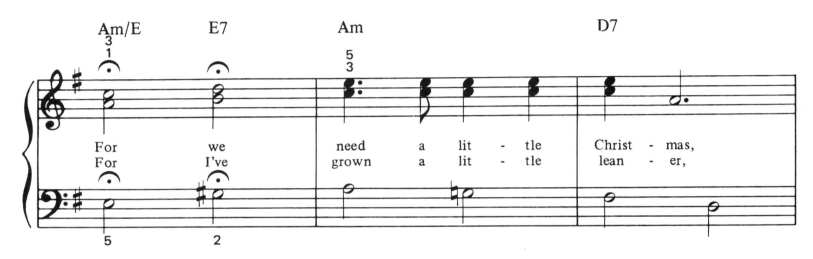

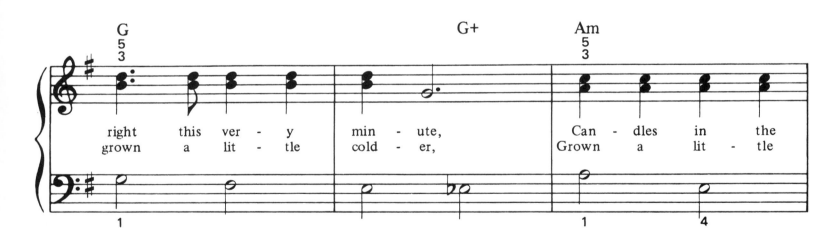

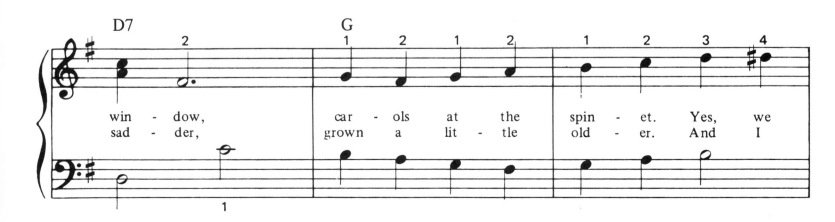

need a lit- tle Christ - mas, right this ver - y
need a lit- tle an - gel sit - ting on my

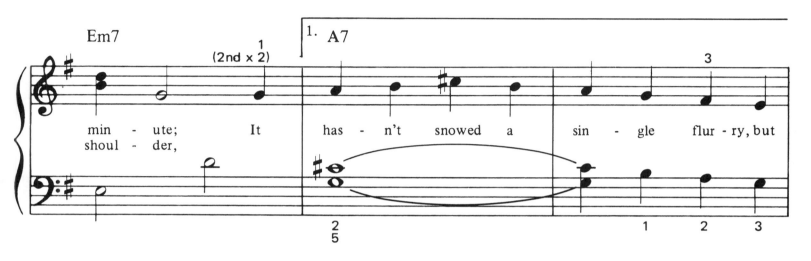

min - ute; It has - n't snowed a sin - gle flur - ry, but
shoul - der,

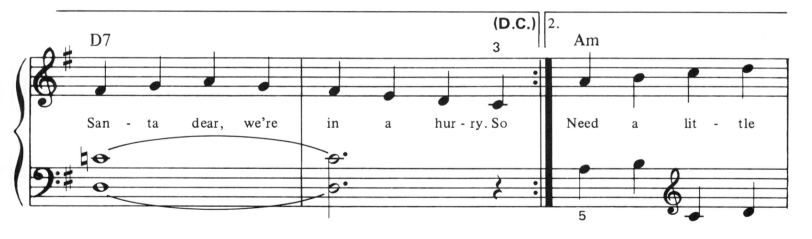

San - ta dear, we're in a hur - ry. So Need a lit - tle

Christ - mas now!

SUSSEX CAROL

Traditional English Carol

WE THREE KINGS OF ORIENT ARE

Words and Music by
JOHN H. HOPKINS, JR.

Gently and quietly

*Implied harmony

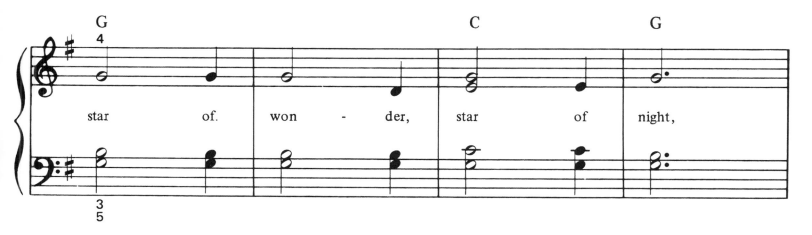

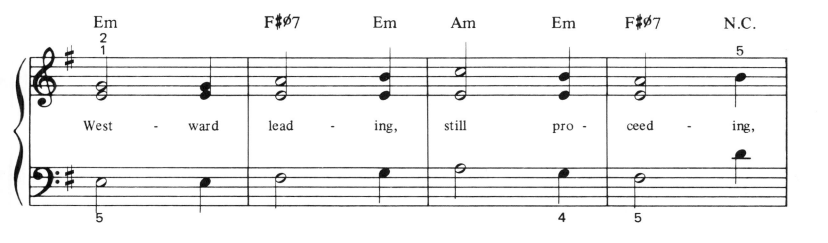

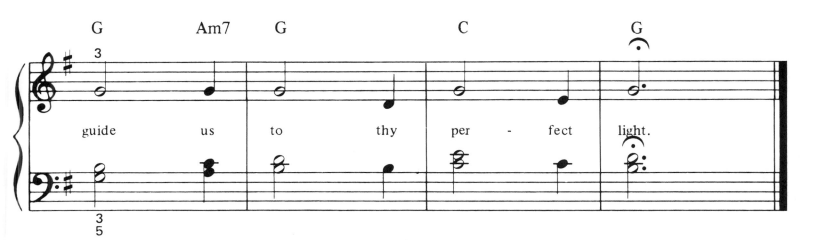

WE WISH YOU A MERRY CHRISTMAS

Traditional English Folksong

WHAT CHILD IS THIS?

Words by WILLIAM C. DIX
16th Century English Melody

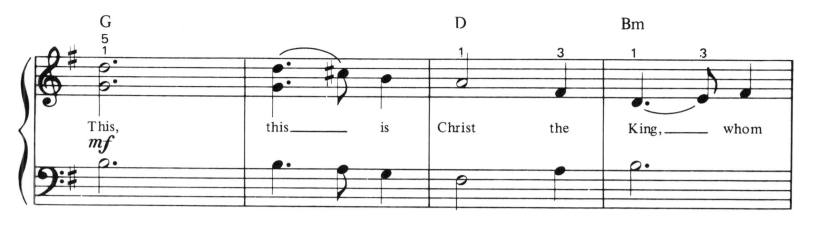

This, this_____ is Christ the King,_____ whom

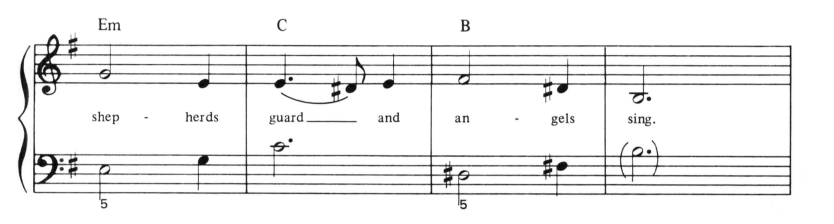

shep - herds guard_____ and an - gels sing.

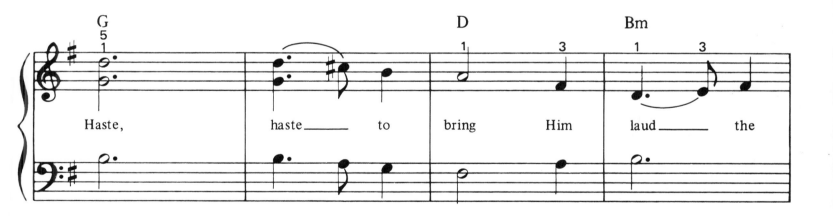

Haste, haste_____ to bring Him laud_____ the

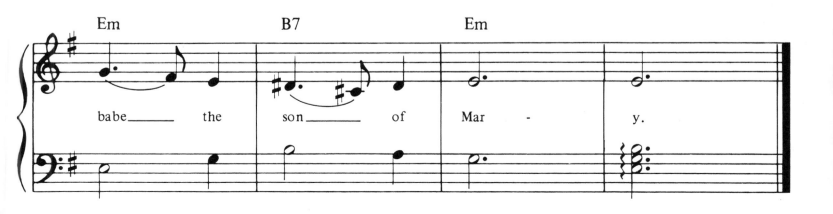

babe_____ the son_____ of Mar - y.

WONDERFUL CHRISTMASTIME

Words and Music by
McCARTNEY

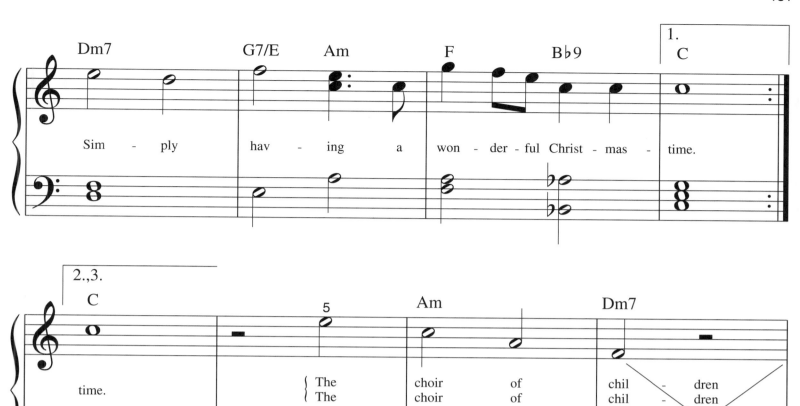

Dm7　　　　G7/E　Am　　　　F　　　　Bb9　　　　**1.** C

Sim - ply hav - ing a won - der - ful Christ - mas - time.

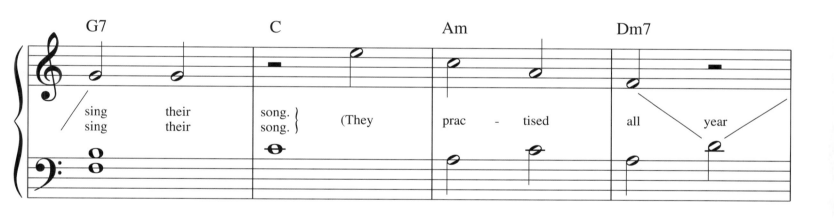

2.,3. C　　　　5　　　　Am　　　　Dm7

time.　　　　The choir of chil - dren　The choir of chil - dren

G7　　　　C　　　　Am　　　　Dm7

sing their song.　(They prac - tised all year　sing their song.

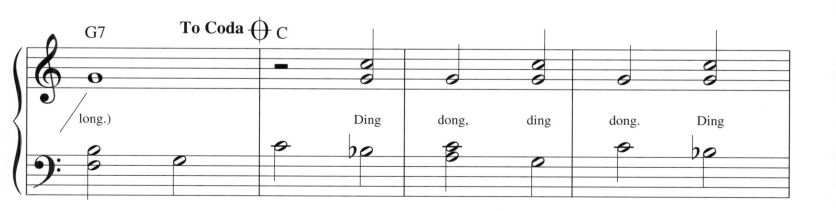

G7　　**To Coda** ⊕ C

long.)　　　Ding dong, ding dong. Ding

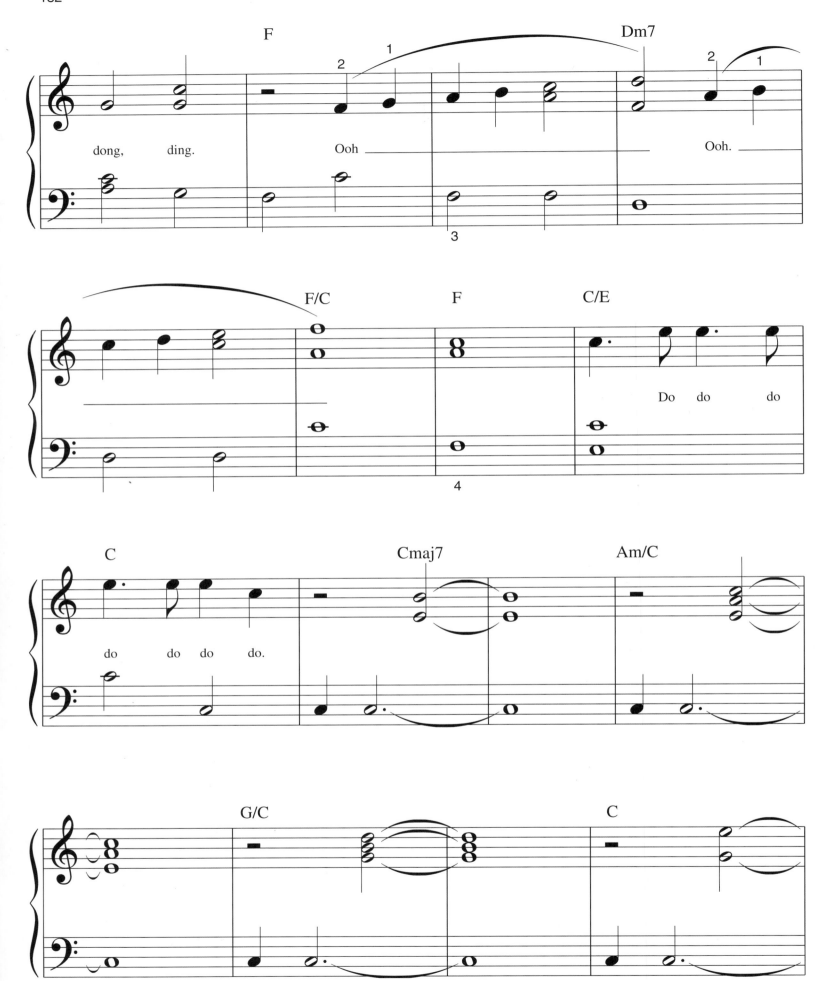